DEFY
EXPECTATIONS

*Learn to Lead with Love,
Integrity and Trust*

HELEN HONISETT

Published by Author Academy Elite
PO Box 43, Powell, OH 43035
www.AuthorAcademyElite.com

Identifiers:
ISBN: 978-1-64085-920-3 (paperback)
ISBN: 978-1-64085-922-7 (ebook)

Library of Congress Control Number: 2019913769

Available in paperback, e-book, and audiobook.

Dedication

For SD & JD, who make me want to be better every day. And for JB, IE, and CW, who force me to be better by always having my back, inspiring me, believing in me completely, loving me, and not accepting any of my excuses.

• • •

When hearts and minds combine, we can all become superheroes.

TABLE OF CONTENTS

INTRODUCTION

This book is about how to lead with both the heart and the head, but the heart first. This book is about being brave enough to be willing to open your heart as well as your head to lead.

Love is the missing ingredient in our corporate culture. We hear a lot of talk about trust, integrity and authenticity in leadership, but without love, none of these are possible. Without loving your teams, your peers, and your mission, you can never truly be a leader that people want to follow. But we never teach people the skill of leading, speaking and working from the heart. We never teach people to be truly open and vulnerable.

This is a book about leadership and team building but it is not your usual management book. I never set out to write a traditional book on leadership as I feel that the leadership philosophies and styles that have helped us to where we are now are not going to get us where we need to get to next.

We see and treat people as units of labour, rather than the critical part of any business that they are. We have undervalued people and the role that their life experience can bring to work, and we have allowed exclusion and elitism to run our boardrooms and executive suites.

What will this book do for you?

- This book will challenge you to think about the type of leader you want to be, both at work and at home;

- Force you to define your values and boundaries so that you know what you stand for and ask you to be brave enough to stick to these;

- Teach you how to love and lead with integrity, along with the trust of those around you in a way that is sustainable;

- Give you the steps you need to take to become and stay truly vulnerable.

Love leadership is not for the faint-hearted, there is nothing soft about love, nothing fluffy. Love is not weak, love is not a doormat, love does not compromise, but love is compassionate, listening and understanding. Love does not sit there with a smile on her face in submission. Love sprints headfirst into action.

To me, love is the ability to see the potential in another, no matter where they are in their journey. What more could we ask from our leaders but to see our potential no matter what?

I am not special or different; I am just me. I have been hurt, I have failed and messed up numerous times, and I will continue to do so. I have hurt others, both intentionally and accidentally. I am not perfect, and I don't aim to be, but I do, passionately, want to make a difference to people and their lives.

I do, however, have over 20 years' experience working, coaching and managing people. I know what works and what doesn't, for the good of each individual, not just the business. I have shown again and again, that by serving and uniting your teams with love, integrity and trust, that you can deliver sustainable business growth.

This book aims to help you in doing the same.

A NOTE ON LOVE

I never set out to write a book and certainly not one on love but here we are, and that is what I have done. There are times when I sit down to write and I am not sure what is going to come out. I have no plan, no structure for the session, and I know I am just being guided to put on the page what I needed to learn or share.

There are also times when I know I need to create a page or chapter that is going to give myself the biggest kick up the backside I can (from a place of love.) This is one of those times.

We are forgetting who we are. We have created so much protection and crap around ourselves that we cannot and will not step back and dare to dream. We spend hours following others voyeuristically on social media to make us feel that we are part of something and we are kidding ourselves that we are living. We are living to someone else's expectations, not our own, and I bet we have not even consciously planned to get to where we are right now. I feel that instinctively for myself. I know there are times when I have deliberately planned, but for most of my life, I have just done the best with what is in front of me. I have done what I think would please others.

We are not living. In fact, we are so disconnected from our life's potential, that love, to us, is senseless. We say love is blind, but for most, it is also deaf, dumb, tasteless, and unfeeling. We commercialise love to the extent that we make it base and purely transactional. We remove all essence of joy from the connection with another and agonise about how we are thought about. Love in 2019 is about image, wealth, and status. It is about being adored and admired. It is not about being known and loved for the soul that you are. It is now about being better than others and that debases love to its core.

We must stop this abuse of love now. We must learn to connect to ourselves and others. We need to grow up and take responsibility for who we are and how we love in this world.

This note may seem like an anger-fuelled rant, and, to some degree, it is. It is an anger burning in me so actively, that I (as have many others) have wasted countless hours, days, months, years, in the pursuit of something so inherent in me and so endless, but I have been blind to it. It is an anger that drives me to write every day about love and the joy it can bring to the world, and it is an anger that has allowed me to tap into the bottomless well of pure love and compassion that I never knew existed. But for that I am grateful to my anger as it fuels me to be a better human being and to have the courage to say what needs to be said.

In love, no emotion is good or bad. In love, our emotions are there to guide and teach us. In love, we can find the greatest knowledge and the strongest fuel. But we must be willing to feel and connect. We must be willing to risk it all for love. Or we choose to live a life of the mundane and senseless. The choice is ours and ours alone. If you are reading this, you are one of the blessed few. You have had an education that has allowed you to be literate, can afford to buy a book and have the luxury and safety to read it. So, let go of your ego, connect to others, and commit to a life that is extraordinary.

But how can we move from where we are now to a place of pure love? What are the steps we need to take and what are the choices we need to make? Love needs trust and faith to grow but not survive. Love can live in the darkest places and exist in the harshest climates but to thrive it also needs to be nourished. We can plant a seed of love, but without mutual trust and faith in each other, it is like a seed with no sunlight or water, dormant and undeveloped because love is about connecting with someone else on the deepest and most vulnerable of levels.

For me, trust is the hardest part of love as it means opening up to the world and volunteering myself up to whatever someone wants to think of you and that is scary. It is frightening to open my heart up each day and pour words on to a page that I know will be criticised, pulled to pieces and debunked, but I have to believe that I am being compelled to write this book for a reason. I have to have faith that there will be one person out there who will read this and be moved.

I am not sure I know how to trust innately. For me, it is something that I have to work on daily. There are times when I am gripped with such fear of putting myself out there that the old bravado flares up and I feel my ego go into protection mode. The habit formed over decades of self-protection, prompting me to disconnect, close down, and I push away. I become sarcastic, I make flippant comments, and I laugh off my discomfort and abject terror of opening up with humour, usually at the expense of myself or someone else.

It is not my intent, but I am human - we are human, and we have programmed ourselves over thousands of years to protect and survive. Our feelings have become part of that. I am sharing this because this book is the scariest thing I have ever done. I started writing it because I felt deep down that there must be a better way for us to lead and manage our lives and relationships at work. For me, that was from love. But this journey has also allowed me to see into the fear and doubt I carry with me. This book has forced me to face my feelings and doubts, over and over again. To realise and embrace my imperfections. It has forced me to question everything and every interaction. It has forced me to look at how I think, act, and interact, in a way that I have run from all my life. This book has forced me to learn to be me. This book demands as much courage from me as it of you I am grateful for this journey, for all the self-discovery it has given and will continue to give to me.

Philip Larkin summed up love in his poem "Verses from Arundel Tomb" by saying:

• • •

Our almost instinct almost true:
What will survive of us is love.

• • •

We live, to quote another poet of another kind, in a material world, where we judge and pride ourselves on our possessions, our status and our appearance. In the age of the selfie, what is on the outside, seems to count for more and more each day.

We need to realise that the only thing that will outlive us is love. I recently attended the funeral of my step-grandmother, a woman I did not know very well but one that lived to 104. The love she had given to the world was evident; felt and remembered by all those in the room and the many other people she has touched across the globe. We will never be remembered for our hair or our sports car, but we will be remembered eternally by the people whose hearts we have touched. Whether it is a fleeting moment where you helped someone in need or a lifetime of dedicated support, affection and love felt by your family; love is all that will remain.

I recall the first time I looked at my mortality. I was in my early twenties and an accident that could have happened to anyone led to the death of one of my university classmates. He was there one minute and literally gone the next, having done something many of us had done on a regular occasion. He had skipped over a fence which was a shortcut home to the Halls of Residence. But this time he slipped, hit his head and that was it. I remember the disbelief initially, followed by shock and then, over the following weeks, the reflection of how little we actually are, unless we are something to somebody. I couldn't grasp how we could be so significant and insignificant, all at the same time. How could I matter and yet not matter? The impact each of us has on the world and our own individual communities seems so disproportionate; so vast in some ways and yet so fleeting in others.

At the time, and for many years, I misinterpreted what it meant to be something to somebody, but these questions lingered with me and it took me over two decades to realise what and who I needed to be. I came across something I wrote in my journal all those years ago recently: "If you want to be someone, be the most loving person in the room. If you want to change the world; love harder. Forget fame or fashion and plump for love instead because when the time does come that you say goodbye to those around you, be it for a day, a week or forever, all they will remember in the end is the love that you shared and the joy in their hearts as they recall how you made them feel."

I only wish that I had understood the profoundness of those words and had listened to myself just a little bit.

My lesson now to others is to never underestimate your ability to impact the people around you and never underestimate your capacity to love.

When I set out to write this book, I deliberated over what I wanted people to do or feel differently having read it. The simple answer I arrived at is that I want you to love more. Even if that means just being kinder to the barista who serves your coffee in the morning or whether you end up changing your entire world to centre around your heart. I want you to love. Love yourself, love the stranger sitting next to you on the train, love your family so much that your heart could bust. Love. Because at the end of the day, LOVE is all there is.

This book is my commitment to love. To bring more love into every minute of every day. To give love more feeling, to be love. I know that I won't be perfect and that I don't always have the presence to practice what I preach, but I will give it my all and my best.

My mission is to make you think, feel and act increasingly each day with more love. I want you to notice it everywhere. I want you to feel it in everything you do. I want you to be eternal through the loving actions you do to others and yourself. Together, by loving more and more each day, we will change this world.

● ● ●

Give yourself the space to be.
In that moment, you will know the truth of your own heart.
Right action flows automatically from a place of divine love and connection.

A NOTE ON LEADERSHIP

I initially envisaged this book to look at how we can bring more love into the workplace, but as I ruminated more on what leadership meant to me, I came to the view that was only the starting place.

The paradigm shift that I want to see in the corporate world is only possible if we are also willing to live from love in every aspect of our lives. The framework and structure of our work lives allow us to decide who we want to be in a relatively safe environment; we can create our "leadership style" in a way that is detached from us as human beings and can be compartmentalised from the rest of ourselves. But that is not leadership.

To lead, you must be someone who can be followed, imitated and who serves others. As a parent, you can choose to guide your children to learn to live a life that helps them reach their potential, or you can just see what happens and go with the flow. As a partner, you can choose to focus on leading the relationship with constant, open communication and discovery, or you can take the safe road and decide not to share your heart fully. As a team leader, you can either inspire your team in a way that serves them on a daily basis to meet their goals and develop their careers, or you can drive them to focus solely on their work, ignoring the critical role they can serve as individuals.

In essence, I realised that leadership, for me, was so much more than how I turned up to work. It permeated every aspect of my life and made me question every decision and choice I wanted to make. How did I act with my children, who was I to my friends and family as well as my work colleagues?

The answer I got worried me. I lead at work but at home, I coasted. I expected to be treated in a certain way but I was not necessarily willing to put the effort into my partnership, and

I did not give my kids the amount of time or attention that I would a junior member of staff. My friends always seemed to fall to the bottom of the "to-do" list. All in all, I needed a significant shake-up before I could claim to be a leader.

This book for me has been a journey into what is truly important to me. What is it that I am going to be most proud of when I look back at my life? There is nothing I can do to change my past and the myriad of mistakes that I have made. But I am fully empowered to live in the present and the future as the leader that I want to be. A person who is brave enough to face my fears and do what I want to do anyway. Someone who loves so hard and deeply that it is palpable. A leader who will tirelessly fight for what is right and to serve those around her. I may never achieve the level of true leadership to which I aspire, but I will not stop trying and striving to be better and better each and every day.

So, if you have picked up this book in the hope it may transform you in the workplace then great, but be warned, I hope it won't stop there. I want you to examine your life honestly. This won't be easy but if you're going to lead you cannot cut your life up into convenient chunks and decide who gets which part of you. You need to go all in, to everything. My journey to becoming a leader started in the office but where it became authentic and real was when it bled into every area of my life, changing who I was at a fundamental level.

I hope this book helps you trust and believe in yourself, dismiss the judgement of others and spread your boundless love into a world that needs your uniqueness and talents.

SETTING THE SCENE

I have come to the conclusion that one of the worst words in the English language is one that we all use daily and it is trapping us at every level. That word is "should". We set ourselves so many expectations with that simple word that we hold ourselves back in chains from everything that we could be.

From the day we are born we are inundated by "should's". We should be born in the right percentile, in a certain way. Then we are measured every day against standards of normality that do not exist. But we are still told that is what we should be doing.

I have lived my life by "should".

I should be an A grade student.

I should be a certain weight and look a certain way.

I should have a full-time job with a regular salary.

I should have a stable relationship and raise kids in a wholesome house in a safe environment that removes our curiosity and desire for adventure.

I should, I should, I should.

I was lying on my balcony in a room in Galle, Sri Lanka, after my first Ironman, when I realised that everything I wanted in life, if I followed the rules, I shouldn't have.

I trained hard for my Ironman 70.3, I learnt to swim, I spent hours on a bike and out running, but on the day, I decided to have fun. I was going to relax into the race and enjoy the experience, not try to break myself to achieve a set a time. For those of you that are not au fait with the lingo, this means a 1.9 km open water swim, a 90 km bike ride, finished off with a 21 km run, all to be completed within 8.5 hours.

I was waving at the divers in the water; I was singing as I swam blowing bubbles to amuse myself. I loudly proclaimed to the world whilst cycling around Colombo that the wheels on my bike go round and round, (the wipers, if I had any, went swish, swish, swish, if you were wondering!) and all I got from my fellow competitors and spectators were very odd looks.

The concept of someone enjoying themselves in 36-degree heat and extreme physical exertion shouldn't be happening. I fell off my bike twice (mainly due to not really knowing what I was doing) and was told I should stop and take a break, but I didn't want to. I wanted to have fun. I smiled at the volunteers and thanked them for their energy, I watched the flying fish as they jumped out of the water in the port (which they did a lot), and I was going to finish. But most people thought I was doing what I shouldn't.

The "run" was fascinating. The number of people struggling in the heat to shuffle in a run-like fashion at speeds that would disgust a tortoise, hurting at every step, some with tears running down their faces, was incredible. These people were miserable, and they had paid to be there. Now, I get the pride of completion and I also get competing for a time, but I don't get that combined with self-flagellation.

I have no Anterior Cruciate Ligament (ACL) in my left knee, which means then when my leg muscles are tired, my knee gets just a little bit wobbly (quite wobbly actually, with a tendency to give up) so I decided I was going to walk. So many people told me along the route to run, I should be running but I smiled sweetly and continued my rather fast-paced stroll around downtown Colombo I finished the race and I had fun.

By so many standard expectations, I thought whilst recovering on my sun lounger; I should not have completed that race. I am overweight, I have a knee injury, I don't know how to get on and off a bike using cleats (hence the number of falls until members of the crowd learnt to catch me!) and I did not push myself. I didn't slack off either, but I was not beating myself to the point of exhaustion and pain. Granted, walking the next day was optional and dehydration caused quite a lot of cramp, but the fun I had was worth it!

I should not have been able to do an Ironman 70.3 in Sri Lanka, but I did. This got me wondering. How many other things should I not be able to do that I could?

I have often been asked in self-help workshops "what would you do if money/time/ability/confidence were no object?" What would you do if you had no limits? On regular occasion, I have tripped out the answers that we should be saying as those are the ones that get the knowing nods from around the room. "Should" has felt like a boot between my shoulder blades pushing me on to meet the expectations of others, and to push me down if I get ahead of myself. On that sun-lounger, I could literally feel the pressure there.

This pressure said I should be doing something. I was in a historic city, in a beautiful country, and yet, here I was, on the balcony of my hotel room, relaxing and lounging. I should be out site-seeing, ticking off places to visit, seeing all the important areas of Galle so that I can dutifully report back that I had done what I should. I should have done a safari; I should have gone and visited the national museums, I should, I should, I should. I was trying to force myself into action. Instead of sitting, being and listening to what I wanted to do.

One of the reasons I think we are so tired all of the time is that we are constantly battling the "should". We drive ourselves to meet the expectations of other people and ourselves in a way that has us in a constant state of stress, fighting or flighting our way through life without stopping.

"Should" allows us to sleepwalk through life doing what we are told instead of what we want to do. "Should" is a cop out and something, that until very recently, I have built my life around.

The concept of this book came about when I realised that I successfully build and lead teams by often doing the opposite of what I should. When it comes to leadership, "should", for me, has never really played a part. I choose people for their attitude, not their skills. I believe in people when I am told not to. I see the criticality of all team players, not just the high potentials and I honestly, and genuinely care for and love my people. I believe that in the workplace, it is a leader's role to create an environment that helps everyone meet their potential and nurture them as human beings, not task orientated robots. I believe in the power of love in the workplace and I have always been told there should not be a place for love at work.

However, love is not a natural topic for me and it certainly is not the logical topic for a leadership book. But the more time I spent in the corporate world, the more I realised that it is the missing ingredient. We spend so much of our lives in environments that are intrinsically designed not to nurture but to conform, not to thrive but to survive and we can see it in every level of society and business. Our media and corporate culture are all doom and gloom rather than grow and bloom. I love working in big businesses; I love the challenge, the hustle, the fast pace, but I also started to understand that it was crushing my soul, stopping me from being everything I knew I could be and wanted to be. Initially, I thought I had to choose, that I could not change such an ingrained global culture - it was me or my corporate career. But, luckily for me, something nagged and nagged until I chose to be different, I decided to be the best version of me, the most loving, the most supportive, at home and, most vitally, at work. That is when my life truly took flight.

I have written this book as a call to arms, to all those who know there is more that they can give. To those who know that by becoming the best they can be means more than learning more management speak or frameworks. For those who look at the talent in their organisation and know that, without a significant change, we will stamp out all creativity and drive. This book is written from my heart to yours, hoping you won't dismiss the longing you have to thrive.

I had a longing, a dream, a lust to build a career and life for myself that I adored, that made me feel good, that surrounded me with people I loved, people I learnt from, people who challenged and taught me, that made me grow, and gave me experiences that I never thought possible. My only problem was that from where I was sitting, this meant working my way slowly and boringly up the corporate ladder, becoming a manager who stuck to planning cycles and word documents, to managing and instructing people.

All my role models had slaved away, had sacrificed, they had never soared through the day on a wave of joy and led with a heart filled with love while at the same time smashing their targets and to-do lists.

Don't get me wrong, working in this traditional way got me to a certain level, but it made me feel stuck. It made me feel as though the conversation I was having with my teams and my peers, were, in essence, worthless. We all seemed to just be going through the motions, never vibrant, never whole, never joyous. My professional development conversations were actions, never dreams. They were how-to-do's, never how-to-feels; they lacked soul. I lacked soul; I lacked joy; I lacked harmony.

There had to be a better way.

Let's be clear, I am not perfect but I am on a mission. I am on a mission to work out how I can be better, how can I love more, how I can I love deeper, how can I love recklessly, bravely, with wild abandon? How can I bring more love and delight to those around me?

To be quite honest, I have spent a lot of my waking hours terrified that I am about to make an enormous fool of myself as I bring my heart to work and talk about love. But I am also willing to stand toe to toe with that fear, look it in the eye and give it a huge hug because it is not going to stop me. Nothing is going to stop me from spreading my message that we need to bring more love into our work life. One of the things that has always fascinated me about a work/life balance is the complete imbalance in love. I tell my family, my children and my friends, that I love them all the time. But God help me if I muttered something similar in the workplace. I would be in the HR office quicker than you can say "harassment". At what point did we decide that we don't deserve to be loved or love our colleagues?

Let's do some maths. If you work between the ages of 21 - 65 for an average of 45 weeks a year at 40 hours a week, you spend an astonishing 79,200 hours of your life at work. That is a lot of time to be spent with people who don't thrill you or support you to be your best. It is an even more significant amount of time to be spending doing something that doesn't make your heart sing! Are we really content to accept and condemn our work lives to drudgery?

Our society has conditioned us that leading from love, be it personally or professionally, is not acceptable. Loving ourselves and others puts at risk the very foundation of our economies - or so we are led to believe. By that, I mean we are expected to do as we are told, stick to our lot in life and not dream of the "so much more" we could be.

We can have consumerist dreams of ownership but not missions to drive a different way of living. But I have found quite the opposite. I have found that leading from love has made me more successful and abundant, whilst at the same time supporting those around me to do the same. It has lead me to engage in conversations many would not. It has taught me more about myself, my family, friends, and my teams, increasing the gratitude I feel for each of them and how they turn up every day.

Leading from love has given me the courage to stand up for my values, to overcome challenges both at home and work, and to ensure that I live a life that I have chosen. It has also given me vast levels of tolerance and compassion for those at a different point in their lives.

This book is about love leadership in every aspect of your life, and it will take you through some actionable steps and frameworks to transform the way you interact with your teams, your peers and your customers. However, for me to be able to set the context of how I came to this path, you first need to know me, my story and my adventure in becoming a global leader, so bear with me as I talk through the main steps that made me a love leader and the tools I used.

My "moment" was not some traumatic event that turned my life on its head and left me fighting for my life, or bankruptcy. No, mine, in a very British way, was over a cup of tea with a newfound friend. She asked me a question, which I immediately dismissed, but somehow got lodged in my soul, fighting and fighting it until finally it got heard. She asked me "Do you want to carry on living with your head or your heart? You are all head!"

Life changing stuff! Huh? Not really.

Over time, however, the question circulated in my mind. It appeared through my meditations, my train journeys or just walking to the shops. My problem was that I had no idea what it meant. I am a salesperson; I am a corporate bunny; I travel the world selling (really important) stuff to people who I think need it. I work in spreadsheets and CRM systems; I spend a lot of time on video calls discussing strategy and transformation. How the hell am I going to live from my heart in a WebEx? So, again, I ignored the nagging feelings and carried on slaving away, pushing and pushing for the next sale, the next target, the next improvement in product or strategy, always looking up at my leaders and superiors thinking, "I never want to be like you, or even have your job, your pay cheque yes, but not your job."

I knew deep down that there must be more, but I did not know what it looked like or really have the courage to take a plunge into the unknown.

During my second maternity leave, I got an opportunity which I thought was the universe pushing me to dive in and turn my life on its head – I got a pay-out – I had the cash to start my own business, to do something new, to do the unimaginable – so what did I do? I started a consultancy that helps people sell better – yawn.

I was so scared about what I wanted to be and do, that I nicely pigeonholed myself into an area that I knew would be ok but one that was never going to change me or my world. I spent days filled with fear about getting a contract in and being able to pay the mortgage until I got offered another job – which I fully justified to myself and accepted. It was a good role, it was security and a pay cheque every month. But this time I knew it was different. I knew I was different, and when I started in my new position, I had made the decision that I was going to be a better me.

Throughout my career, I have had some incredible mentors, people who truly believed in me and my talent, but I was always encouraged to play it safe. It was not about reckless joy but regulated ambition. Keep small, keep delivering, be a good girl; the promotions and rewards would come. To be fair, they did, but it always felt at a compromise of my passion and the scale of my ambition. I know that sounds arrogant and I don't mean it to. I am actually not out to find glory, but I am out to change this world. That is what drives me; to make this place better and better for everyone in it. Playing small was not going to cut it anymore.

At the same time as my redundancy, I came across a guy called Brendon Burchard – if you have not heard of him go Google – he is (for a Brit) quite cheesy, but get past that, and he rocks. Within the first two minutes of one of his YouTube videos, I had made a decision. "I want to play bigger!" My head had finally caught up with what my heart already knew - there has to be more than this.

Granted, I am already top 10%, I earn a very good salary, live in an awesome house, and am mum to two of the cutest kids around, but now I was going to step it up a gear. I was going to become my best "me!" I was learning framework after framework; I was chunking my day, I was becoming uber-productive, but was I mattering?

One of Burchard's questions was "Did I matter?" Again, no thunderbolt moment but the question spoke directly to the one stuck in my soul. "Do you want to carry on living with your head or your heart?" And my soul screamed, "I want to live from my heart!" at about 1000 decibels.

OK.

Problem.

I have no idea how to live from my heart. I have no idea how to run a workshop on financial planning from "my heart", I don't know how to lead a Google Hangout "from my heart"!

But I had made a decision, and with that, the veil dropped. I finally saw that to be the person I wanted to be, I didn't need to sell all my worldly possessions and live in an Ashram chanting all day. I didn't need to become a vegan, tee-total, sanctimonious or dull. I could be me. I could lead sales calls. I could manage huge teams across the world. I could do drunken Karaoke with customers. I could continue to climb the corporate ladder, but do it in a way that made me feel good, that made me want to open my heart to all my colleagues and customers and love them. I could look at my sales forecasts with joy and gratitude, to deliver an organisational transformation that was filled with love and acceptance, even of those who would no longer be in their jobs. I had decided to lead from, and with, love.

I still didn't know exactly what that meant, I was still figuring out whether that changed anything I actually did or how it would change the world, but I did know it had changed me and at that moment that was the only thing that mattered.

I have not had a tough life, I have had it easy. I am blessed, privileged, born in the west and incredibly well educated, but I still struggled. From a very early age, I struggled with my self-image, with who I was and how I fitted into the world. I never felt that I was a fit anywhere. I never felt that I belonged. I always questioned why people would be friends with me, so I bought people's affection (mainly with alcohol when I was younger), I used my younger brother to find friends, I hid, and I protected myself from the world so that I never had to engage. If I didn't feel that I belonged, then I was damn well going to ensure that I couldn't be hurt either. When I look back, I was always doing something but never actually present, never in the moment, never truly happy because I was never truly me. I thought being me was unacceptable. I did everything to conform, to make people happy, to please others.

I am from a family of achievers and the response to "what are you going to do with your life?" could never be "happy." It had to be bold, ambitious, and require you to earn lots and lots of money. You could only be happy with lots of money because "money gives you choices." So, every choice I made was based on how much it was going to earn me. What do I do for my A levels? The things that will make you a doctor because doctors earn lots of money – ignore the fact that physics and chemistry bored me to the point of complete disengagement. Never mind the fact that I have never actually wanted to be a doctor – it would make people proud and earn me money and if I had money then, of course, I would be happy.

Following the money has done me well to a degree. It has spurred me on to keep pushing, to try harder, to prove that I am worth the pay rise or the bigger bonus, that, combined with a natural talent to sell, has led me to be very successful in the eyes of many, but it has never made me happy. Figuring out what makes me happy is tough and is an on-going process that requires letting go of so much baggage and endless self-imposed expectations, but it is worth it. I have had to make tough choices and learn what it truly means to be an adult. I have had to go toe-to-toe with friends and family to stand up for what I want, but I know my happiness is critical to me being the person I am here to be. It has been and will continue to be a constant voyage of discovery and self-reflection.

My journey of developing myself as a leader started in 2006 when I moved to France. I was coming out of depression over the loss of my grandfather. I was going cold turkey from the antidepressants and I was hiding. Big time! Hiding from the fact that I didn't know myself, hiding from the fact that I felt a failure following my depression, hiding from the fact that I had run out of ways to lie to the world about how blissful my life was. Worst of all, I was hiding from myself.

I lived in a beautiful town called Sauveterre de Bearn, near the Pyrenees. If you have never been to this area of France - Go! It is a beautiful, picturesque gem, hidden between the glitz of Cannes and the old-world sophistication of Biarritz. The Pyrenees are awe-inspiring – not because of their size or the amazing (lack of) skiing, but because of their energy. They make you feel small and significant all at the same time. They resonate with a past that has held legendary secrets, caused wide-spread struggles for power (think the Cathars and the Pope), and have also been a sanctuary to those who have needed them. It was within that energy that I learnt I could look inwards. I could step back from the face I was bravely projecting to the world and interrogate my fear, my past, my behaviour, my "me". However, I was going to do this in a very logical, contained, compartmentalised, and, if possible, fast way. Or, to put it another way – I was going to do this from my head.

LEARNING

It has been my belief that you cannot love someone unconditionally until you can love yourself unconditionally. Don't get
me wrong, you can love deeply, powerfully, in a way that turns
your life upside down, but you cannot love unconditionally until
you love yourself fully and madly. This does not stop you from
loving but getting to that point of unconditional acceptance and
love takes work on yourself as well as work on how you treat and
interact with others.

Learning this lesson has been tough for me. I have always
seen others as better than me in nearly every way imaginable, so
getting to the point where I can honestly say I love myself has
taken more than four decades, many wrong turns and a serious
realisation that perfection is an impossible target. Truly loving
yourself is one of the hardest and bravest decisions to make. It
requires the courage to look into the eyes of your deepest demons
and uncover all the baggage you have been carrying around for
years. It means embracing your flaws, forgiving yourself and, if
my journey is anything to go by, bawling your eyes out on numerous occasions and punching the crap out of some cushions.

I cannot say I am there. There are still some days when I am
not as kind to myself as I could be or days when I still snap at
myself and others, but I am light years better than I was and I
see this as a lifetime of lessons and endless practice - I am not
going to wake up one morning and know I am done but as long
as I can honestly say I am getting better each day, that is enough
for me. I am also more tolerant of others which is an additional
benefit of loving yourself; it is easier to love everyone else.

My biological father left when I was very young (about 20
months old), and for years I reasoned that because I was so young

there was no way that it could have impacted me. Wow, I was wrong about that one!

It was not until I saw a friend of mine play with his young daughter, that I realised how close that bond is so early in life. Once I had had kids of my own, I fully understood the devastating effect that his departure had on my heart.

My father just vanished, and, at a very young age I, unconsciously suffered and shut down my heart completely. It was never a decision I made, but it was one that went on to impact my life significantly. Shutting down so young made it very easy for me to brush over any effect that this abandonment may have had. The wound was so old and so deep that it felt like a birthmark, something I had been born with. The defensive mechanisms I put in place to protect me were automatic, a habit from birth, but it led me to disengage from everyone around me and created a deep-set numbness that I thought was normal.

I was never unpopular at school, but I was never the cool kid. I was never the brightest, but I was never an under-performer. I just floated numbly through every experience because I felt I had to and I never felt that I belonged. As long as I had the stamp of approval, by doing as I was told by those around me, that was enough.

The memories I have of my childhood seem very detached, as if I am watching a movie of someone else's life, not my own. I didn't engage, and I didn't connect, I just went through the motions. I could detach at will and even cut people out of my life cold from a very young age, unaware of the effect that it had on others, only seeing how it was protecting me.

I drifted through secondary school miserable and heavily bullied but too scared to say anything, as I was sure I didn't matter to anyone. I searched for any group that might have me, but in the process, only damaged myself further. I suffered from Bulimia for years attempting to fit the mould in any way I could. I joined the Christian group in a hope they may let me in, only to be bullied more. Every holiday I went home with a smile on my face, determined that my parents would never know a thing. I would not be a burden on them or get in the way of their lives.

If I am honest, there were times when just ending it seemed like a good way out but I was lucky, in a sense, that I never got further than self-harm and an eating disorder.

I may be sounding flippant, but I still find it incredibly challenging to look back on those years and not feel as though my heart is going to break, partly from the memories of the pain I went through but also from the knowledge that I did this to myself. I know I was a child and I did not know better, but I was the one who made these choices, I was the one who was not brave enough to say what I needed and when. I spent years and years torturing myself and I have continuously repeated this pattern. One of the reasons I am so keen to share everything in this story is not to hold anything back, so if one person reading this realises for the first time that they are not alone, then I have achieved something with my life. This book is not about fame or fortune; it is about helping people realise that the best they can be is themselves.

By the time I got to university, I had become so shut down that when people stopped being impressed with the amount of wine I could buy them, we drifted apart, or worse if they really did want to get close, I ran, and I ran fast. Protecting myself became the most critical driver in my life, ensuring I could maintain the mask and keeping everyone as far away from the real me as possible, was everything.

There were times when I sensed what I was doing, but it was much easier and safer just to move on to the next group of friends, and then the next set of friends, and so on - you get the picture.

In the summer of 1997, I discovered recreational drugs, nothing very hard-core but enough to drop my guard a bit and it was one of the most memorable (or not) summers of my life.

It was, undoubtedly, the starting point for me allowing myself to get to know me. I actually had fun, real fun, not the fake fun I had been pretending to have all these years. I had moments where I stopped checking to see if I was pleasing people. I discovered I could let myself go, even for a moment, be it on the dance floor or just being myself in a conversation, without feeling that people were going to judge or criticise my every move. I discovered having fun.

I also discovered serious hangovers and the determination to still deliver a great day's work on three hours sleep (a skill that has served me well with travel and small children), but when you are young, that is all part of the game.

I had found a tribe, and I loved each and every one of them. They were wild, they were fun, they were caring, they were mischievous. They actually liked me and I believed them. But once the summer was over, I headed back to university and unconsciously expected that to be that. Mobile phones were only just starting to come in and staying in contact was not easy. However, every time I went home, they were there, and they were always thrilled to see me. I remember finding this tough to deal with, the more people showed me affection, the more my inner voice screamed at my stupidity, beat me up for my imperfections and told me that none of this would last.

So at the end of my degree, I decided to travel; to run away from these people but to do it to a place with cheap beer, gorgeous beaches and long bus rides. So, I packed my bags for South East Asia. It was not a conscious decision to run away, in fact, I thought I was being brave and adventurous, but I now know that I was not ready to face being part of something.

Asia inspires me. I have always felt at home in this vast continent and most of this book has been written whilst travelling in Asia. The irony of my running away to a place that felt like home only hit me many years later, but being in such a foreign place allowed me to be detached in a safe way. In a culture you don't know you are automatically an outsider, and that suited me just fine.

Every week was an adventure with new faces, places and currencies, and I could again hide behind a mask. For me, one of the joys of travelling is that it is transient in nature. You are allowed to be there one day and not the next. No one will find it odd if you just vanish, in fact, they will praise your free spirit. So I fitted right in! I travelled around countries that had so much to offer, that I could experience without having to engage at any depth. I could move around as an observer, never connecting, never being.

To give me a reason to be away for so long, I started volunteering in local schools, the more remote, the better. The reason (I needed a reason!) was so that others would not think I was wasting my life and education. I did not feel that I was able to choose how I spent my life. I felt guilty that I was not out there pursuing a career already and climbing the corporate ladder. I knew I wanted to do something different, but I had no idea what it was or how I could do it without letting people down. It took me until my 40s to figure that out!

So, I ended up in villages in the middle of nowhere in Cambodia and Thailand, attempting to teach English to people who had barely seen someone as blonde as me. I spent my evenings communicating through mime and sign language with villagers who saw me as a novelty. It was beautiful in its innocence but incredibly lonely in its existence. It was in these remote places where I started to understand the healing power of nature. Loneliness became a catalyst for me asking myself why I did not want to be with people, but also why I was so uncomfortable being alone. Without distractions, I started to listen to myself in a way that I had never done before and what I heard scared me.

To this day my favourite place on earth is sitting on a beach under the moonlight, listening to the waves crash in and out, counting the stars and feeling the magnificence of Mother Nature. My first forays into meditation happened on such a beach, but I did not know at that time that that is what I was doing. We can so easily get distracted by our day to day lives that we miss the significance of the world around us. The constant noise of our lives can separate us from the calm of nature. The non-stop pace of city life can consume us into thinking we permanently have to be in a state of "Go!"

When was the last time you watched the wind move the leaves on a tree, or saw a snowflake float slowly to the ground? Or stared up at the stars for a minute more than you usually give yourself? Engaging and contemplating with our surroundings is a huge of part becoming present and in the moment. On the beaches in Thailand, I started to connect with my surroundings and myself. I began to see that I was part of a bigger whole, that I was actually part of something.

In Thailand, I fell in love with scuba diving and with the fact that I could hide in a different world. I remember lying on my back, staring at a number of fish playing above me, cut off through a lens of glass, utterly dependent on my tank to survive, and thinking to myself "this is how I have lived my entire life – completely disconnected."

Having spent most of my life in a state of hyper-vigilance, being in an alien environment gave me the freedom just to be and enjoy. It also allowed me to be curious, to explore, to sometimes push the limits of what I could do and what I could see underwater.

On paper, scuba is one of the weirdest things. We strap enough lead to ourselves to make us sink, whilst at the same time wearing a device that is designed to make you float and carry a tank of air on our backs, just so that we can explore a world that could kill us without all this paraphernalia.

But it is worth it. The weightlessness of being underwater and the sheer beauty of the life there is awe-inspiring. Spending time staring at a reef is a lesson in inter-connectedness and inter-dependency. Everything has its place, from the tiny polyps of coral to the sharks that cruise the edges. Nothing is surplus or a burden to the ecosystem.

The profoundness of my thoughts underwater never hit me until I re-read my diary from that trip, nearly 15 years later. But it did start me questioning if living with such a disconnection from the people I loved was what I really wanted. What I realized is that I wanted to learn to love and to allow myself to be loved by them in return.

So, I headed home.

Love had always been a strange concept for me. My grandmother and step-grandfather were so dysfunctionally obsessed with each other, that they had more or less cut off their children. My grandfather and step-grandmother never showed any affection, and my mother was at the end of her second marriage to an amazing man and father, but, I had never seen real love.

Love to me was physical and transactional, which quickly translated in my mind to sex. The more sex, the more love – right? Quite a simple equation and one that when you are blonde, bright, young and sexy, you can balance nicely and very successfully.

So, my desire to learn to be loved quickly turned into my desire to make love - not the healthy or the healing transformation I was looking for. Looking back, I know that I could never actually have understood what it meant to love without understanding what it meant to trust, but that is part of the story that comes later.

It worked well for a while until I met someone who really cared for me. It was also about the right time for me to settle down, move out of my mum's flat in London and become an adult. Or so the narrative of my mind-written story dictated. I had had my fun, I had seen the world, and it was now time to pay back the investment in my education and to prove my tax-paying worth to society. So, it was time to conform to the norm and get a guy, a job and a mortgage.

He was also one of the summer of '97 group. So, not only did I quickly end up with a fiancé who loved me but a group of friends as well. To be honest, it wasn't all bad - there was a lot of laughter, fun and community, but I never felt I belonged, or that I was doing anything that I was genuinely passionate about.

We got married in a beautiful ceremony that I helped to write, in a place I truly love and we were surrounded by people who were thrilled. I just felt numb, but I knew what I was expected to do – by this point, I had had over two decades worth of practice. I could convince anybody of anything. So, I dutifully walked down the aisle on the arm of my step-father, signing up for yet another role that I was not convinced I could play.

However, I did have one ray of light. It was also at this time that I realised I was better than most at sales and that I could throw myself into the workplace and excel in a purely functional way. I could thrive in an environment that has never truly valued the human soul, I could carry on hiding and become successful doing it.

So, there I am with a husband, a mortgage, two cats, a good job, newish car and a deep-set terror that this was my life. Now, please do not get me wrong, my ex-husband is a kind, loving and nice man, but I could not truly love him because I could not truly love myself. I had a man hell-bent on loving me, but I fought and fought to keep him away. He talked about our retirement, of walking down a beach hand in hand together in our 70s, and my mind screamed with terror. We avoided any conversation about children and I even got him to agree that we never needed each other. I think it is fair to say that if anyone could have actually seen into my heart, they would have known it would never last, but I know how to put on a show, and to the outside world (including him), we were happy and the "perfect" couple.

The impact of the lie I was living, on others around me, was again, something I did not understand. I knew I was not who I wanted to be, but I did not see the devastating effect it was having on the people around me. There was no way anyone was going to walk out of this unhurt in the long run, but I was blind to see that and unable to even consider speaking up for myself. I did not see that my lack of courage not only hurt me but every-one around me.

The facade worked until 2005. On my first wedding anniver-sary, my wonderful step-grandfather, Alan, dropped dead entirely unexpectedly. My world fell apart, and I had no idea how to deal with it.

I still miss him every day. The 31st August each year fills me with a combination of profound sadness that Alan never got to see me become who I am and meet my children, and joy, at the fact that I had someone like him in my life.

But by the time I had heard the news, and travelled to be with my mother and brother, they had started on the wine and the gallows humour. Instead of doing what I needed to do (cry and cry a lot), I joined in. We buried him in June, but I didn't cry until September. By this point, I could not stop. I was not sleeping, I had lost all energy, I was going through every day as a complete zombie. I was even more numb than before and completely shut down – I was now clinically depressed.

I can remember Googling the symptoms I was experiencing, and depression was consistently the answer. I was horrified I was that weak. How could I have got to this point? How could I have let myself be this stupid? How could I be this ridiculous? Why couldn't I just pull myself together like normal people do? I had an internal voice that went on the full rampage. How dare I be so weak and pathetic to be depressed? Did I not realise how lucky I had it? Did I not see the burden I was on those around me? I was useless, worthless etc. etc. etc.

Just to set the record straight, I do not think depression is a sign of weakness. But my inner voice did. The part of me that was going to judge and beat myself up in the cruellest way did, and it was going to let me know.

At that time, my father-in-law was living with us. He was not a healthy man, in fact, he had spent many a decade successfully pickling himself in a mixture of vodka and cider. To the point that at his cremation, there was a sharp intake of breath from the packed-out room as he entered the furnace – we were all slightly fearful (and hoping) for an explosion – he would have loved an explosion!

Anyway, my father-in-law was ill, fatally, as it turned out, but his presence, whilst from one perspective was adding to the pressure, it also made me realise I needed help and fast. I did not want to end up living a life like his. I got myself an appointment with our local doctor and was prescribed anti-depressants – cue internal monologue going in for another beating!

Accepting that I was depressed was one thing, having to go into work with a sick note and a prescription for drugs was another. I was brought up to have a stiff upper lip, we didn't complain, and we certainly weren't weak or vulnerable. I can remember being told by my grandmother that "I had it good and I should be grateful for what I had". Though that is undoubtedly true, it is not particularly helpful when it comes to caring for yourself or your own mental health.

I remember feeling and knowing that I had let everyone down. I had become weak and no longer useful. After I drove to work on the day after my doctor's appointment, I sat in the car with the sick note in my hand, dreading the conversation I was about to have with my line manager, knowing she would judge me as pathetic and no longer a worthwhile member of her team. After about 15 minutes, I plucked up the courage to open the door and walk into the office. To give everyone their due, they were all wonderful and supportive, but I was in such a dark place, all I could think of was how quickly I could get out of there to avoid the judging looks I was getting. As so often is the case, the worst criticism and pain came from the voice in my head.

I decided to take the drugs. Even that was a battle I fought with myself. I have a degree in Physiology and Pharmacology, so I know about the chemical imbalance that can be triggered to lead to depression. I know that one of the most effective ways of dealing with acute depression is mild anti-depressants, coun-selling and exercise, but I was not going to listen to sense if I could beat myself up. But I took them, finally, and they helped. I started to sleep, I stopped crying, but I was also numb, and I knew I could not heal if I was numb. I needed to feel the loss of Alan, I needed to scream and shout at him – he had left me when I needed him, and he had left me on my wedding anniversary – the bastard always had to have the last word! I knew I needed to feel, but all I could do was get through one day to the next.

At the time, my husband and I were talking about taking some time out to travel and get me well again. Alan had left me a bit of money in his will, and we knew that we could use it to make a change in our lives. We spoke about backpacking around the world, living on beaches and exploring new continents, but we settled on moving to France.

So, we packed up the house, put everything into storage, crammed a tent into a Ford Ka and headed South.

CROSSING THE CHANNEL

The song goes that when the going gets tough, the tough move away as far as they can…well, not quite, but I was definitely trying to play tough, and I wanted as much distance between me, and anyone who may be able to see through my facade, as possible. South West France may not be the most obvious choice, but with a 14-hour drive and a reliance on RyanAir, it certainly ticked a number of boxes. It was also convenient and far enough at the same time. There is also something wonderfully isolating about being in a country where your grasp of the language is "schoolgirl" at best. But I could not get away from myself, and that, luckily, proved to be my downfall.

We spent three months camping in a beautiful part of Southern France, settling into the routine of local life, and, changing the pace of ours significantly, we decided to start a business. The plan was to buy a house and start a life running holiday cottages. Now, anyone who now truly knows me (of which there are now a few I am pleased to share), would giggle at the concept of me hosting holidaying families and being happy in a small town of a thousand inhabitants, but that is what we decided to do. Even buying the house was a battle. If I had known then what I do now, I would have seen that the number of obstacles being put in our way was the universe saying "stop" very loudly. But I had a goal in mind and nothing was going to get in my way. Determination and bloody-mindedness were going to get me back on my feet and being successful again! (I am so glad I can now laugh at myself!)

But one of the issues with having a part of you that self-bullies is that you do not ever want to be alone – ever. You do everything you can to make sure that you don't get stuck with that inner voice. I had tried alcohol, huge transient friend groups, one-night stands, anything to make sure that I spent the minimum amount of time "toute seule". But the reality is, that in order to love yourself, you have to be happy sitting by yourself, you need to enjoy your own company. It is tough to love someone you don't like, not impossible, and we will come on to that, but tough, and really tough if that person is you. This is where I learnt about the art of meditating.

I had successfully run away from my support network, placed myself in a village where I did not speak the language and laughably thought I was saving myself. But the universe has a great sense of humour, and all my logic and determination had landed me in a place where I could not hide. But the universe is also kind, so I soon found people around me who had the skills and willingness to teach me how to deal with me.

I know that every book you pick up nowadays tells you, you must meditate, and to be honest, yes, it works for me, but so do long walks in the country, running so far and fast that you want to puke, and singing my heart out whilst simultaneously dancing round the kitchen. But most people plump for the former as you get fewer strange looks when practising in public places.

My relationship with meditation has been hit and miss; sometimes it flows, I can fit it in my schedule and other times it just never happens for months on end and then stress, self-doubt and fear come and smack me so hard on the arse that I have to stop and listen. However, over the last few years, I have got to the point where if I don't meditate on a daily basis I can now sense the difference. I am not able to focus as well and I get stressed more easily.

There are people out there who are far more qualified than me to teach you how to meditate, there are YouTube videos, free apps and sessions in your local Buddhist temple, but the most straightforward thing for me is my breath.

I had heard about meditation before I moved to France but had never considered it beyond lying flat on my back trying not to snore at the end of a yoga class. But it was in my garden in France that I first started to give it a go. Most people will tell you it takes time and patience to really experience anything when you meditate, but for me, it was an instantaneous view into the infinite possible. I think I was so numb and tired that I wasn't expecting anything. I wasn't trying and I had no knowledge or expectations of the life-affirming joy meditation could give me. So, when this overwhelming sense of peace descended, I honestly did not know what to do except sit there and smile.

For the first time in over a year, I was feeling something. When I look back on it now, I can put words around it like "source energy", "pure joy", "the vortex", or whatever new age metaphor you want to sign up for, but for me, back then, it was so pure and peaceful.

All I was craving was peace and a place to rest. Striving, beating myself up, trying to be perfect and running away is exhausting and I don't think I had understood how exhausted I was. I was at breaking point, well let's be honest, I was past breaking point, and I was a mess. I was overweight, coming off anti-depressants and so unsure of who I was and what I was worth, that any kind word or action was rebuffed and scorned. What I felt sitting in the garden was a breakthrough.

I think we misunderstand peace. I certainly did. I think we equate it with calm and even being a bit boring, but it is the most energising and healing state I can be in. When I am at peace, I am in the flow, I am centred, I am present, and this is where healing can really take place. I remember sitting there on the lawn, breathing in the fresh air, feeling the sunshine on my skin and letting peace envelop me. I was not after a lightning bolt moment. I was just after a sense of ease; I just wanted to let go, to stop struggling. I was after a place where I could allow my soul and body to relax and renew. With that renewal came a hunger to learn more. To understand how I could reach this state more readily and also how I could learn to do this all the time.

It began by meeting a woman who gave me a book called The Journey by Brandon Bays. To this point, I had never been spiritual. I had once gone to church quite religiously (excuse the pun), but mainly so I could use it as an excuse to go to the teenage church group in the nearby town on a Monday night. When, what I was actually doing, was going to a local pub and doing the quiz! But engaging with spirit, engaging with a deep well of joy and love was not something I was going entertain.

Until that point, being spiritual meant one of two things; you were either one of those happy clappy crowds who to me seemed elitist and exclusive or an anti-establishment hippie wandering around in too much tie die. Spirituality was not something I realised we all need. We all need a way to connect with our souls, to the piece of you that is uniquely you.

I liked The Journey – it was logical, it followed a set pattern, and it allowed me to play the system. I could get good at "Journeys". I could do what was needed, I could be seen to be developing, recovering, learning to be "good", but I never actually needed to let anyone in. You are facilitated through the Journey process but you never have to explain yourself, and if I was candid with myself, after the first couple, I worked out I could detach myself from the process to a degree and go through the motions, rather than delve into the emotions.

It was safe, and I didn't have to be vulnerable, I just had to say what was expected to be heard – so I dived headfirst into The Journey. I attended workshops. I went on long weekend retreats to learn more. I made comments that made me look good to the rest of the room, I spoke about my personal growth, I longed for the moment when I would wake up one morning, be a size 8 and I never had to worry about anything else in my life again – coz of course miracles can now happen – I read it in a book. And thus, my exploration into the world of self-help and spirituality started.

Next came a movie called "The Secret." WOW! I can win the lottery overnight; I can create car parking spaces; I can build a miraculous life by just using my thoughts. Hey – that's easy – I have another tool my head can use. I know I am sounding cynical, but at the time, each step of discovery I took was actually significant, taking the next step is the critical part, and it is not that I am cynical, but I have become a little jaded of a production that was not open about the hard work, soul searching and time I really needed to commit to learning to be a better me. It all sounded too good and too easy to be true.

The main message of The Secret is that our thoughts create our reality. So, for a thinker like me, this was great. I could use The Secret to think my way into a life that others would be envious of. I can live from my head and never have to touch all those gooey, uncomfortable, messy feelings. I can maintain my mask and do it all whilst fantasising about how I am going to spend my 100 million pound lottery win – Hallelujah! I focused on creating something that would make others look up to me or even proud. I never allowed myself to use any of the techniques I was learning to figure out what I truly wanted or who I truly wanted to be.

But life was going to be great!

For a while it was. To be honest, The Secret for me was a Godsend. I had, by that point, created an astonishing and ter-rifying inner monologue that would make hardened criminals collapse in tears and rock back and forth in the corner calling for their mummies. If I wanted to find someone who could tear me a new one, all I had to do was listen to my internal voice.

I don't know when I started to internally abuse myself, to me it seemed that it had always been there. I was worthless, nothing, fat, ugly, unlovable, pointless, insignificant, etc. etc. etc. – this voice could go on for decades! Without that movie, I am not sure I would have ever noticed it. For me it was normal and I truly believed it was normal. I also truly believed and felt everything it said.

But for the first time I was aware, I was listening, and I started really listening - not necessarily changing my belief of the words that were said, but I actually gave it time and then changed what I heard. I became conscious of my thoughts, and I think, at that point, I became conscious of my life, my ego, and my baggage.

Acknowledging that voice and the fact it was ruling and ruining my life was the start of the fight back and was my first step into being able to let it go. I would even go so far as to say that I was actually able to love it and laugh at it. Acknowledging that voice was my first step to leading a life full of joy and love.

Controlling my head and changing my thoughts was one thing I knew I could do, so every day I picked one phrase from my inner diatribe, wrote it down, and then I wrote the opposite. For example, one of my favourite songs on repeat was "I am useless". Not at anything specific, I just believed I was generally lacking in "use". I started writing a list of things that I am quite useful at: cooking, selling, drinking (that got dropped from the list quite quickly for obvious reasons!) working hard, chatting to random people - you get the gist.

Once I had a new list of the useful traits, I started repeating them to myself like a mantra, over and over again until they felt natural. Very slowly the list of repetitive thoughts changed from nasty to normal, and I started to feel that I was slowly putting myself back together, in a way I had never been before.

But I was still hiding from the bigger demons, my emotions and how I valued myself. I was doing a very good and useful job of papering over the cracks. But it was at least some long overdue renovation.

For nearly five years I lived in France, perfecting my ability to drink red wine with the locals, hosting wild parties and renovating French houses, but I was ultimately still hiding from baggage I needed to face. My relationship with my husband was falling apart, and I was throwing myself into yet another corporate job I had managed to secure. No matter how hard I tried to maintain the status quo, I now knew that the universe was going to continue to put me in to situations I did not like until I learnt my lesson.

• • •

I did everything wrong in my marriage from an unconditional love perspective. I wanted someone who worshipped and adored me, but I also wanted someone who I thought I was better than. I didn't want someone to love; I was just so terrified of being abandoned (again) that I wanted to make sure I was with someone who I knew wouldn't leave - at least not physically. As I write that, I know how awful that sounds. The man I married was a wonderful guy with great talents and depths of love and affection, but I just wanted someone there who would put me on a pedestal and tell me how great I was. If that ever faltered, I became a nightmare to live with.

Unfortunately, this happened quite regularly. I was holding him up to my unreachable expectations of perfection that, at every point, he was destined to fail.

I am not proud of the person I was, but when I look back at the lessons I learnt, I am pleased I went through the experience. My love in every aspect was conditional, and if conditions weren't met, I pushed back and acted out. I was a spoilt brat, acting like a three-year-old who wasn't allowed yet another episode of "Paw Patrol". Whilst I am the first to admit that I have not thoroughly learnt this lesson, I am now at least aware of how tough I can be to love and live with and to be honest, I am continually grateful that people are willing to put themselves through the pain.

I created scenario after scenario where the poor guy was set up to fail. To prove to myself how right I was that no one could love me or treat me how I wanted to be treated. I hated myself so much that I made sure that anyone foolish enough to fall in love with me would sooner or later come to the same conclusion; I was unlovable. I pushed and pushed until my husband shut down. He emotionally stepped away from our relationship and I had the proof I needed.

Ending our relationship was one of the hardest and easiest things I have ever done. I was so convinced that anyone in my life, who did not have the misfortune to be related by blood to me, would eventually leave, that the final push came simply. However, the hardest part was that I not only isolated myself from someone who loved me but also everyone else in my life. I had proven myself unlovable, so that is what I became. I am amazed, truly grateful and humbled, that anyone from that period of my life still talks to me. Not many do, but still, more than I would ever have expected.

Inner misery and self-hatred came very easily to me. I, still to this day, have to catch myself every so often, as I can again, slip into that habit under stress. The balance of my inner beliefs and trying to meet the expectations I thought others had set let me spiral out of control. I vividly remember one night sitting in the flat I was sharing with my brother, by myself, finishing an entire litre bottle of vodka, neat.

Standing up, I walked to my bedroom, entirely steadily and put my hand out to grab the doorknob. As I did, I noticed that I was not shaking, that my vision was not blurred, and I was not what I would consider drunk. It was then I realised that I had a serious problem.

Interestingly, not with alcohol, but with myself. Unless I did something drastic to stop my habits, I was going to kill myself. I know that may seem overdramatic, and I don't mean I was considering suicide, although that had been something that had occasionally crossed my mind ever since my teenage years. But I was abusing myself so severely that, inevitably, at some point, my body would say enough is enough.

My marriage had ended, and with that, I had lost both my husband and my closest friends. I had pushed my little brother and mother as far away as I could, I was working every hour I could, and drinking like a fish.

Alcohol has always been there my entire life, and it has been an easy tool to use for self-abuse when needed, but I have also been lucky enough that stopping has never been an issue. I can and always have gone for weeks at a time without a drop, or had a glass at dinner, or significantly more on a big night out but it has never been my addiction, and for that, I am eternally grateful. But if alcohol was not my problem, but my crutch, then what was my issue? How was I going to heal something I couldn't even name?

The reality was that I did not have a clue what to do. I didn't know how or who to ask for help and I was 100% positive that if I did, no one would come. But I did enjoy yoga, so I signed up for a yoga retreat in Ibiza, run by a friend of a friend. That decision turned out to be one of the best I have ever made in my life. I had been here before, at this breaking point, and the last time I ran to France, but this time I knew I could not run again. I needed to stay and face whatever this was; I needed to grow up, take responsibility and get my peace back.

I had got to a point where I knew no one but me could change where I was or how I was feeling. I don't think I had ever classified myself as a victim as such, but I had been waiting for someone to rush in and make everything better. The irony about that is I know I was not willing to ever let anyone in, so no one would have been able to help anyway.

A yoga holiday seemed to tick a number of boxes, it was an opportunity for "me" time without going on holiday alone and I could even get some time in the sun.

The retreat was centred around a combination of Bikram and Kundalini Yoga. Two massively different types of yoga, but precisely what I needed, and both had me curled up in tears sobbing my heart out on a yoga mat on nearly a daily basis.

I love Bikram yoga; I know many disagree. But for me, the absolute necessity to be in the moment and to concentrate on your breath to even get through a class without passing out due to the heat, forced me into both the present and my body.

Bikram studios are also usually surrounded by mirrors, so there is no escaping yourself. Any hang-ups you may have about your body are there for you to face head-on in very sweaty real-time and you have to look yourself in the eye to get the concentration and balance you need for most of the postures.

I have never noticed how I avoided doing this at all costs. I could not hold my own gaze. I could not look myself in the eye for more than a couple of seconds without the desperate need to turn my head and hide away. The problem with that, is that you tend to fall over in Bikram if you lose concentration. I had 90 minutes every day where I had to get comfortable looking myself in the eye.

The guilt, the grief, the hatred, the sheer despair that I felt about what I had become, tore through me and repeatedly threw me on my arse, literally and emotionally. How could I ever forgive myself or even like the person I was? The sweat and tears poured freely as I tried to figure out how I could get through to the end of the sequence, let alone the end of the day.

Facing myself for who I was is one of the toughest things I have ever done. I had become a master of deception. Putting on a facade for the whole world that I eventually believed it myself. I had no idea who I was, what my values were, or how to be me. Getting to the point of acknowledgement was a huge step, but only the first in what I now consider to be a lifelong journey of healing.

I had never been nasty on purpose, it had all been about self-protection, but the reality was that I had hurt many people around me and was continuing to do so. I was manipulative, self-centred and controlling, all so I could cover up how scared and alone I felt. I was not living, I was coasting through a blessed life, and I was squandering the opportunities that were being given to me.

Between these vicious self-torture sessions in a hot yoga studio, we spent the rest of our days relaxing in the beautiful hills of Ibiza and it was here that I read a poem that started to change my life and my relationship with myself.

The Invitation by Oriah Mountain Dreamer starts with the lines:

• • •

It doesn't interest me
what you do for a living.
I want to know
what you ache for
and if you dare to dream
of meeting your heart's longing.

• • •

The lines spoke straight to that part of me that was aware that I needed help even after I had drunk all that vodka. It spoke to the part of me that still longed to live. It spoke to the part of me that ached to live and dream and be. In that moment of healing, that week I had let myself feel part of myself that I had shut off so completely. I had connected with the part of me who dreamed of belonging, of being, of being worthy enough, to love and to be truly loved. It gave me hope.

I wanted to know what I could dare to dream if I let myself. I gave myself permission to start letting go of all my expectations and try to discover who I was. In reality, it took years for all those expectations to truly dissolve, but that was the point that I decided they were gone. And that was all I needed to do. I needed to give in and listen to what I really wanted and stop fighting to maintain and control my mask.

The other practice on the retreat was Kundalini Yoga. I think it is fair to say that Kundalini is still a branch of yoga that is not mainstream and it is considered a little wacky by most, but I was here for wacky, and I had had a bit of exposure to Kundalini when I was in France. I was delighted to dive in and see what would happen.

One of the core aspects of Kundalini Kriyas is the repetition of a movement, and the magic happens in the repetition. Like Bikram, this was a practice of concentration, devotion, and, more often than not, a desperate plea to oneself to just make it through to the end. The idea is that during movement energy starts to move around the body, releasing blockages and emotions that you have stored.

And, boy, was I releasing! I have never cried as much or healed so much in such a short period of time. Having never really let myself express the negative emotions I had a lot stored up, crying alone or, God forbid, in front of others, was not something I felt I was "allowed" to do. Tears are a sign of weakness; they show a lack of self-control. That was how I had been brought up, but the need for tears and release was starting to become apparent.

Crying is one of the most open, honest and vulnerable things you can do. I still struggle with crying in public, I have decades of programming and a British culture that is not comfortable with displays of negative emotion, but it is sometimes the only way to engage with how you feel when you feel it. I cried and let go as much as I could.

The flip side was, that I finally understood how hurt and damaged I was. The deep black chasm that I had been ignoring all of the pain I had stored and inflicted on myself was going to have to get dealt with. I understood that I could not deal with years of physical self-harm and emotional abuse, from myself and others, in a one-week retreat. This healing was going to take years and patience. Patience has never been my strong point.

When I got back to London, my ego roared up and demanded that because I was so damaged, I deserved to be treated like a goddess. I had pushed my relationships to the max already, and now my ego was in full battle mode to ensure that I would stay as disconnected as I possibly could. Everyone had to bend over backwards for me, or they were not worthy of my company or my time. If I did not feel that I was the centre of someone's attention I moved on.

Online dating let me use people like toys, I would play with one until I got bored and then move on, casting people aside like rubbish. I set ludicrous expectations of perfection and discounted anyone who didn't fit my ideal. Bitterness and pettiness made me justify how I was treating people and the hedonistic lifestyle I was leading.

Looking back on how I behaved coming out of a healing environment, like the retreat, has fascinated me, once I was self-aware enough to notice. The pain and self-compassion I had initially felt, turned on its head the moment I got back to my daily life. Humility and understanding were replaced by a driving need for acknowledgement from others. I seemed to want those around me to pay for the pain and hurt I had, mostly, inflicted on myself. My agreement to take responsibility for myself and my life disappeared in a flash.

Taking responsibility, or being an adult, is tough. It means admitting your mistakes; it means being open and vulnerable, it means facing the fact that you are not perfect, have a lot to learn and it requires effort. Quite simply; it is hard work and most people can't be bothered.

It was back on my yoga mat during a morning Bikram session that I was knocked on my arse again. I was in one of the standing poses when I looked myself in the eye, something I had avoided doing since getting back from Ibiza, and I didn't like what I saw. There was a hardness, an anger, a viciousness that I did not recognise or like, and I instantaneously understood what I had read, so many times, about the ego. Part of me was purposefully disengaging from healing and life.

Part of me was so wrapped up with what everyone else thought of me that I had become hardened and created a new version of me that was bullet-proofed - and not in a good way. I remember being so focused on my own eyes that I literally keeled over and the shock brought me back to the moment.

I have always struggled with the concept of self-care, as it has often felt like self-pity or a waste of time, but at that moment, I realised I needed to look after myself before I lost myself. I felt that I was at a crossroads, one way would take me down a road which may create a life that looked great from the outside but would leave me constantly alone and unhappy, or I could choose to give myself a break and look at what really made me tick. I needed to learn what made me happy and I made a choice.

To this day I am still questioning myself at every turn to truly figure out what makes me happy. We are given so much programming throughout our lives that it is easy to slip back into someone else's expectations or definition of happiness but making that choice to question everything opened up a strength in me that I did not know existed. But I felt it immediately.

So little is known about how the power of our being can influence the world around us, but that week I had tapped into a well of incredible strength and compassion. It was a force so strong, that nothing, not even my ego, was going to get in the way of the healing path I had to embark on. It gave me a determination to find out who I am.

Looking back into my own eyes, I stood up on the mat, moved myself back into the yoga position and silently told myself "I love you".

I love you. Three such small words, but words with the power to change the very nature of your being and the world around you. The sacred simplicity in these three words can change how you feel instantly. For me, hearing them makes me feel safe, empowered and special. Feeling the power of these words hit my body, gave me the strength to step up to my ego, give it a hug and thank it for helping me realise, yet again, that I had a lot of work still to do to learn to become the person I wanted to be.

I walked home that day through the city of London, and I vividly remember the vibrancy and the beauty of the day and people around me. It was like I was seeing my home city for the first time. I was experiencing its energy and heartbeat afresh. Us Londoners claim to be a grumpy lot, but all I saw were people filled with love, hope, ambition, joy and enthusiasm. I started to see through my eyes, not through the filter of my expectations or prejudices. For a very brief moment, my ego had taken a break, and I saw the world for what it is; a place filled with abundance.

Egos don't give up easily, and it was not long before I was back at my desk behind my facade, but that experience started a new habit. After each yoga class, I would head home really seeing and feeling the world and each time the sensation lasted a little longer. Eventually, I could tap into that place on demand. I had learnt how to get into the moment. I had found the power of now.

There is so much written about the importance of the moment and being in the present but the one thing I had never understood, until I felt it, was the fact that expansive, endless, eternal and boundless love can only truly be experienced in the now. The instant you feel your heart swell and your lips turn up into a gentle smile is when you are experiencing the moment so acutely that the joy overwhelms you.

Learning this skill does not mean that I wander around in a blissful state of "nowness", I had not become some serene guru overnight, but I had given myself a tool that I could use to come back to myself, ground myself, and pull myself out of the maelstrom that my life can quite often become. I don't think we are meant to float around in a single state. I believe we are here to feel, to experience everything: the good, the bad, the ugly. To use these times to learn and develop. To decide on the life we want to lead and the choices we need to make to do just that.

The present is where unconditional love lives, the moment you move into the past or the future you end up with expectations and conditions. Living in the moment is tough in today's society, we have so many mediums that clamour and fight for our attention, that stepping back into the present requires discipline and awareness. Human beings love distraction; it can give us a false sense of security and comfort. Acute presence seldom means facing physical danger anymore, but it often means facing emotional dangers. You cannot bury and repress your emotions in the present moment, they roar at you, demanding to be heard and felt, and that can be enough to knock you back into the comfort of the past or the fantasy of the future.

But the trick to dealing with any emotion that comes up is to stay in the present. Emotions are fleeting; it is only our ego that builds them up and allows them to last more than an instant. The best teachers in dealing with emotions in the present are children. I have watched my sons, with awe and curiosity, deal with a range of powerful emotions in a flash. The intensity is incredible but so is the speed. As we grow, we are urged to dampen our emotional responses and store the outburst. Let it out instead! How we deal with our emotions are a choice, we can either: bottle them up and let them build, or we can express them in the moment and experience the freedom of release.

I wish I could live in the present more. It is not something I am brilliant at; I am not sure anyone is unless they dedicate their lives to the pursuit. For those of us with a day job, a family and a social life to juggle, it is not always easy to be 100% present. But it is an art that I am in a daily battle to perfect, although I concede that I most probably won't manage it in this lifetime!

AM I COMFORTABLE IN MY SKIN?

I was just thirteen. We were visiting my grandparents in Warwickshire for my grandmother's birthday. I was so proud of how I looked in my new Laura Ashley dress (back in the 80s they were cool!) and I can remember playing with my cousins, chatting with my aunt and generally enjoying myself, when my grandmother announced to the room "Helen, you are fat, boring and ugly."

I can remember the silence. I stared at the stripes on my new blue dress and wished that the ground would open up and swallow me whole. I remember the complete bafflement as to where such a comment came from. I remember the hurt and clenching my fists so tightly, my nails digging into my palms, as I pushed down any reaction, and pushed back my tears.

After what felt like a lifetime, but was most probably just 30 seconds, the noise of the room returned as everyone went back to what they were previously doing, apart from me. I sat there on the old red brick hearth, still staring at the stripes on my dress, not knowing what to do. No one came to see if I was OK, no one said a word to me for most of the rest of the day. It was like a declaration had been made. A statement had been aired and no one was going counteract it.

A rip had been formed between me and my family, and my self-image lay in tatters. I could not understand why no one stood up for me or at least came to my side. I came to the conclusion that that was what everyone thought and, therefore, it must be true. I am fat, boring and ugly. The interesting thing was, that not only did this have the foreseeable impact on my self-esteem, but it was another subconscious lesson to me that when I was in need, I could rely on no one but myself. My father leaving, my grandmothers' proclamation, and a number of other incidents, left me knowing with every cell in my body, I was here alone, and that was that.

It was one hell of a way to start your teenage years.

Now, my grandmother was beautiful. Movie star beautiful - she was even in a movie with David Niven called A Matter of Life and Death. In my mind, she was clearly in a position to pass judgement, that judgement had been made and who was I to disprove it. I accepted it as the truth. And this truth stuck with me for over two and a half decades.

I had never had a comfortable relationship with my body. I was bullied at school because of it and it took me a long time to forgive it for letting me down. I was bulimic for many years, starving and abusing my body as much as I could, as I believed my body was working against me, and if I could have, I would have abandoned it a long time ago. The constant internal battle and disconnection between "me" as this entity that inhabited this gross physical vessel consumed my life. I honestly thought I was alone in my hatred and fury of myself. So, to drown out these feelings I turned to food. It is rationally oxymoronic, to loathe your body because of the way it looks and yet repress these feelings by stuffing your face with ice cream and cheese, but it seems to be the globally accepted coping mechanism.

I always thought I was alone with how I felt about myself, but the number of people who feel a similar way is genuinely shocking. Even though in the toilets of my boarding school there were notices on the doors, politely asking us to tidy up after we were sick and to open the window, I was oblivious to the fact that others were suffering as well.

I am not sure that I would have recognised kindred spirits back when I was a teenager, as I was so absorbed in my own experiences, but as I have grown up and started to examine my feelings around my physical form, it has led me to have conversations with friends and strangers that have left me in tears. The grief and the guilt I felt for having systematically abused my body took me years to release.

Writing about my body in a leadership book may seem unrelated at best, but as a woman brought up in our western society, my body and my self-esteem are intrinsically linked to how I perceive others will judge me. Whilst it may be a sweeping statement, it is certainly true for me, I have held myself back because of how I think I look; I am too fat, too blonde, too young, and I think many women (and increasingly men) do the same. We let our physical form define who we are at home and work. We so easily and quickly judge others based on looks first. Thus, becoming the leader I wanted to be, also meant me getting over all of my hang-ups about how I looked and forced me to come to terms with the baggage I had, quite literally, been carrying around for a lifetime.

Our bodies are here to allow us to enjoy life and live it. They allow us to touch, hear, see, taste, and smell the incredible world around us, though the majority of us seem to spend our time at war with the very tool we have been given to embrace these experiences with. But our bodies do not define who we are.

It has been very recently that I have understood what a gift my body is. The gratitude I now feel is overwhelming and healing.

Have you ever felt your toes? I don't mean touched them, but have you ever closed your eyes and really felt your toes? Felt each one as a separate and unique part of your body, explored how they steady you and move independently? I bet the answer is no. Most people don't experience their body or life through their body; they tend to engage with life despite of it. We are so used to being told over and over again by the media, our friends, and ourselves, that our bodies are not good enough, they don't conform to the modern-day concept of beauty, and are, therefore, worthless.

Even companies who sell themselves because "you're worth it" are selling products designed to make our skin look more flawless, our hair thicker, or our lips more luscious. I enjoy makeup, but I am equally comfortable without any. I am not going to tell you that in order to love yourself and your body that you have to denounce all beauty products, but what I am saying is that you need to be using them because you want to. Not because you think you will be judged negatively if your pores are not fully minimised or the dark circles under your eyes are not concealed.

Every day I become more and more appreciative for this body I have been given, for all the things it can do, and sometimes can't. I wish I had learnt this back in my youth. I certainly don't consider myself old, but I guess out of my 42 years, I have spent at least 35 of them worried and concerned about my body, and what people have thought about it. What a waste of my time - I could have been having fun instead!

That's the irony; we are given a body to allow us to experience life to the fullest and yet, we spend our time limiting our enjoyment because we are concerned about our body and how it will be perceived.

We need to stop feeling ashamed or embarrassed about what we have been given and instead embrace every unique feature, every different curve or crooked part. We need to celebrate our uniqueness more and dismiss the need for conformity and uniformity. Start by telling your friends, your family, your children, and yourself, how beautiful they are. Let them know how you love the way their eyes sparkle when they are excited, or how the sound of their laughter makes your heart sing. Tell them you love the way the light catches their hair or how their smile lights up their face. Start telling people the things that you wish you would have told yourself. Start being the person in the room that embraces all the unique and wonderful things about the people you love.

Being a leader people want to follow means putting yourself out there. It means taking risks and standing up for people who may appear lacking in another's eyes, and that opens you up for all sorts of criticism. If you are not comfortable in your own skin, it will be very obvious to those around you and make it hard for you to stand your ground in the spotlight, if you need to. Now you can fake it, I have done so on a number of occasions, but I have also found that I have become more authentic and effective now that I don't have to.

As a female leader, I am often told I am a role model to the younger women in the organisations I have worked for and this has always thrilled and terrified me in equal measure. I love the fact that I can inspire others, but I am also aware of how many imperfections I have and the number of times I have winged it or failed, but then I have to remember that that is how I learnt and how I came to be in the position I am in. I am now grateful that I have learnt to accept who I am, and whilst I would have loved to have got to this point in my twenties and not wasted so much time on focusing on the wrong things, I know it takes time to accept who you are, for who you are.

Getting to this point of acceptance has been something that I have been sweeping under the proverbial carpet for decades. I struggle with my weight, but I would never have considered this an issue about love. I would have blamed genetics, bullying, not giving too much of a damn about fitting a societal stereotype, but self-love and care; no.

It was a journey of pain and discovery to understand how I can pull together all the different parts of me to become the leader I wanted to be.

My body and I have not always got along, in fact, there are times when I have abused it to the point of collapse, and I still have to be acutely aware not to do that again. It is not that I have actively sought to destroy it, but rather that I think it is a tool for me to use how I see fit, and therein lies the problem.

If I don't care about my body, then how can I truly care about myself? Our species has this amazing ability to distinguish between the physical and the sentient. We can separate ourselves from these vehicles which move us around and allow us to interact with our environment, and whilst that has led to some astounding discoveries through thought and discourse, it also feels that it gives us a copout when we have to deal with the whole of ourselves.

When I started writing this book in January 2018, I was significantly overweight, but that was not a factor by any means for me beginning to explore love and leadership. It was a significant factor in my self-resentment and cropped up every so often in my self-beratement, but I was used to that noise as it has been there most of my life.

What I did find fascinating was that as I started plunging myself into looking at the role of love more closely in everyday leadership, I started losing weight.

Every time I addressed another deep-seated issue, a few more kilos would come off and then I would stall. I could stick to eating plans and exercise, but only if I was actively sticking to dealing with my issues as well. It took eight months for me to make the connection intellectually. At some level I knew, instinctively, that by fighting my demons, I was also fighting the bulge, but it was not until I had plateaued at a weight for a couple of months and found my eating habits going off the rails again, that I started questioning why it was so easy earlier on in the year and seemingly impossible now.

I started looking at what I was doing when losing weight seemed effortless, and the most substantial change was writing this book.

At some point in May, I stopped writing.

I cannot tell you why, or even if it was a conscious decision, but every evening as I went to bed to settle in and write another section I would stall, become distracted or convince myself that I was far too tired to be creative and my head hit the pillow instead.

I think I was scared. We were in the process of getting ready to move to a new house; I was coming to terms with the fact that I was a mother and a fiancée, and I was not sure I wanted to be either. I wanted to run and I wanted to hide; continuing to write about how love infiltrates my life on every level felt like lying.

I was feeling trapped and suffocated in a life I had built but was not sure I wanted. Again. Had I not learnt from the past? Had I not made the conscious decision to have children and say yes to my partner when he proposed? HAD I NOT LEARNT? And what was wrong with me??

There are so many people in the world who are not blessed to have the life that I lead. The couples I know who struggled and fought to become parents, whereas it seemed to happen to me overnight; twice. The singles who dream of a partner as supportive and as tolerant as mine. But I felt trapped by normality and conformity.

But that is a terrifying prospect to live with and impossible when you have children. I decided I had made my bed and I needed to lie in it. My weight loss stopped, too.

Now, I get that equating a life-altering admission of not wanting to be a mother to losing weight seems trite and insulting to those involved, but what I started to understand is that my body is a physical representation of me. When I want to hide emotionally, the fat appears (or does not budge). When I am feeling brave, with a willingness to approach and address my problems out in the open, the fat slows dissolves, allowing more and more to be revealed.

I have now reached a place where I love being a mother, but the self-doubt and questioning that happens when you take on parenthood seems to be yet another taboo subject. I felt like a freak for airing my feelings publicly.

I recently admitted to my colleagues, that I am everything that was expected of me, but not what I wanted or want to be. My body seconds that; I was my grandmother's expectation of me: fat, boring and ugly.

I committed to myself in the mirror on the evening that I finally put two and two together, that I would continue to write. To get down on the page everything that was cropping up for me and hope that overtime it would form a coherent narrative and force insights that can help me address my biggest fears and my weight, once and for all.

Do I love my two boys? Yes absolutely. Do I find being a mother the toughest, most exhausting, expensive, overwhelming, and disarming thing I have ever done? Yes. Would I do it again? I don't know. I love my boys, and I decided to have them, so I will be the best mother I can be and that does mean being honest with myself and them. I have noticed that with this acceptance has come a joy in being a mother, a joy in not knowing what I am doing, a joy in learning in every minute how to raise two humans to be the best they can be.

Does their father understand? No. The kids to him are everything, they are what he always wanted, but I also know that he finds fatherhood exhausting and overwhelming, as well. But somehow that is OK. It seems OK for a man to struggle with parenthood, but when I mention my issues, they are either laughed off or met with stern, severe faces. I have even been asked a couple of times if I am suffering from post-natal depression, which seems to be a well-worn copout of tackling tough and uncomfortable issues about motherhood. "Don't worry about that crazy one over there, she just depressed" is the undertone from many I speak to. Well, I am not, I just don't think motherhood is the blissful bed of roses many people make it out to be. Most minutes of most days it is exhausting, trying and repetitive. I don't find it mentally stimulating but there are shining moments that make it utterly worthwhile.

I don't feel that I am listened to, but I also know I am not the only one out there struggling to be the mother we are all expected to be.

IS IT SAFE TO BE THIN?

I have been asking myself this question for a while. As I dive more and more into my emotional baggage to build the courage to live the life I want to, it has become clear to me that it was not. Well, not for me, anyway. The thought of being thin scares me. It opens up so many risks. It leaves me vulnerable to the attention of people, of both sexes, it opens me up to comments and it takes courage to set boundaries.

Having been in the corporate world and sales most of my career, I have been privy to my fair amount of sexual banter. I can't call it harassment as such because, whilst it made me feel uncomfortable, I could always hold my own, and I never felt unsafe in the moment. But what I am now discovering is that the fears and insecurities I shut down, were done so with over-eating.

There are a number of points in my life when I was healthy, athletic and the right weight, but each time I stopped exercising, started over-eating and shutting down. I have always put this down to my lack of discipline and weakness, but having stepped back and started looking at timelines of each of these cycles, the one thing that happened every time was that I began travelling or spending more time with a new group of competitive and ambitious male colleagues.

I like men. Most of my closest friends are men; I am more comfortable in their company than with women, the majority of the time. However, spend enough time at a bar with a group of blokes, and at some point, there will be the odd comment here or there. Either aimed at a pretty barmaid or colleague. Sub-consciously, I quickly picked up that it was not safe to be thin and beautiful in this environment. Sooner or later, I would get objectified and not taken seriously.

I would rather be taken seriously than be thin and healthy. It is a vicious circle of external validation. I want to be taken seriously so I make myself as unattractive to men as I can by putting on weight. But I also want validation from men, and one of the easiest ways to get that, is to be attractive to them. But I am not as I am overweight, so I then beat myself up about being overweight and put on more weight, until my environment changes and I can calm down, start to feel safe, validated, and then the weight comes off. But the comments start again, so I start to feel nervous and afraid again, seeking sanctuary in food, and the cycle kicks off once more. In an insane motion that is not only dangerous for my health but also my sanity.

As the obesity crisis continues to grow in the West, is there a connection with how much we have opened up our self-esteem to external validation through social media and comparisons to unattainable ideals of "normal"? Have we created this situation, not through the over processing of food, as it is now also possible to get more healthy choices than ever before, but via a combination of impossible benchmarks, withering self-belief, the acceptance of criticising, and competing with others? If we learnt not only to love ourselves completely but others more openly and fully, could we avert a major health disaster as well?

I am not a scientist, I have no proof of a definitive connection between weight and health of one's self-love, but I do know that for me the link is undeniable.

The times I love myself less, I treat myself worse, and that means more food, more drink, and less exercise.

I have made the decision that I want this circle to stop. I am actively looking for ways to be more vulnerable, to surface my fears, to understand my triggers. What have I soaked up subconsciously that is now ruling my life? What can I expose and let go of to give me the freedom and fitness I so crave? How can I become the awesome, inspiring, and loving human being that I want to be? How do I let go?

• • •

I found that, as I started to dig deeper, a lot of my issues were based in anger. Anger is both a blessing and a curse. It can drive us to right the wrongs that we perceive in this world, or it can drown us in a sense of victimhood that can stifle our appreciation of our lives and the opportunities we have all around us.

I was scared of anger for many years; it seemed to be an emotion that was taboo in my environment. The assumption was that it led to confrontation and my mother avoided confrontation at all costs. I learnt to as well. I bottled it up. I used it as a shield to protect myself from the world. The moment something happened that I didn't like I got angry, jumped on my high horse, proclaimed that I was such a victim and that I deserved so much better. The truth was, I was afraid of facing my anger and letting it guide me to the answers I needed to hear.

When I see anger in people now, I know that what they are actually saying is "it's not fair". Anger is based on a feeling of injustice, either to our egos or to the greater good. If it were not for anger, women would not have the vote. If it were not for anger, we would not have eradicated segregation of races from a number of countries in the world. We still have a long way to go, but anger has led to some of the greatest changes this world has seen for the better. It is just a case of how we use it.

Loving your anger can seem bizarre at first. It takes time to sit with your anger and dive into it, to understand the root cause, to distinguish between ego and a connection to the source of the energy that drives betterment for all. No emotion is good or bad; it is how we respond and act based on that emotion that determines the outcome. That was a tough lesson for me to comprehend as it is so much easier to compartmentalise into "good" and "bad". Labelling seems easy, but we all know that placing a label on anything can define and limit it. By labelling my anger as "bad", I limited my ability to use it in a positive way and, by thus, I limited myself.

One of the things I love about anger is its speed. It can come and be released in an instant if you are open to let it flow.

We need anger in our world to power us to greater heights, to stand up for others, and our beliefs. We need anger to cleanse injustice and prejudice from our actions and those of others, and we need anger to allow us to be brave enough to face our fears. But we also need to be able to recognise the difference between the anger of our ego and righteous anger.

Ego anger usually flares up when we feel that something or someone has belittled us. It is the anger we feel when we get annoyed at the person jumping the queue or cutting us up on the road. Ego anger is a good indication that we have an issue about ourselves that we need to deal with. Whereas, righteous anger compels us to step up, to act, and then speak out, often in a way that we did not think ourselves possible of.

My wells of anger run deep, and the two, ego and righteous, regularly are intertwined, making it hard for me to distinguish between the two. The anger I feel towards my biological father and my maternal grandmother for the way they treated me, fills me with such rage that there are times that it would be easy to descend into ego and victimhood. Yet, that anger burns as strongly to remind me how I want to treat and raise my children. It reminds me of the tenderness and support I lacked growing up, and it makes sure that I commit every day to never, ever, allowing my children to experience the abandonment and harsh criticism that I did.

We always have a choice with anger; it can control us or drive us to be better versions of ourselves.

In his book, "The Power of Now", Eckhart Tolle talks about the observer. The part of you that watches you be you. It is a strange concept at first, but can you ever remember a time when you were acting from a strong emotion; such as anger or joy; and you caught yourself thinking about how you were acting whilst you were also simultaneously doing. I regularly experience my "observer" when I am caught up in stress. I can hear myself saying out loud to someone that I can't do this or that, or that I am so busy, etc. whilst the quiet voice in my head is telling me simply that all I need to do is meditate and take some time out.

My observer is the part of me that helps me keep out of ego anger. When I feel the anger flare, there is always that quiet voice telling me to proceed with caution. To not get swept up into the burning rage but to wait, just an instant, to hear what this anger has to teach me.

The best example of this hesitation making such a difference in my life and my relationships is with my boys. There are times when our children push every button and stretch our every limit to the point of snapping. For me, it is usually when they are not doing what I am asking them to do, but are being fun-loving, in-the-moment kids. I feel the anger rise, "why aren't they listening to me?" my inner ego anger screams and just as I am about to yell at the top of my voice, the quiet voice tells me to breathe. Am I really angry at the kids or am I just exhausted and in need of a bath and an early night?

That instance is the difference between two upset, hurt and crying children and a guilt-ridden mother, and a fun-filled evening, where I can laugh at their high-jinks, let go of the small things and the need for perfection and relax into being the parent I want to be. At work, it is the difference between a snappy and short conversation with a colleague and a powerful discussion that can lead to increased trust and development.

I don't find this easy, in fact, I find it exhausting and one of the hardest things to do, but I know that I need to be able to read my anger. This is not about controlling it. I actually want my kids to know that anger is OK to show, but it needs to be understood as you do. I don't want them to repress their anger, as I did so much growing up, that they carry it around for decades before learning to let go. I want them to feel the burn of their anger and to understand what it means and how they can use it to be the best versions of themselves.

My anger has also been the barrier to me connecting with others, my security blanket that has kept the world at an arm's length, the aspect of me that allows me to seem intimidating to others if I want. It gives me armour and a hardness, and it has been tough, scary and frustrating to let go of. In a way, I am grateful for it as it has kept me safe, but it has also kept me playing small, it has stopped me from trusting others, and it has stopped me to truly loving and being loved.

Learning how to be with my anger has allowed me to open up so much more. Loving my anger has required me to cultivate my observer, and as that muscle has grown stronger, I have noticed that it can connect with other emotions, such as joy, in a way that gives me more balance and understanding. I lived a life where I would dwell and stew on the negative emotions I felt throughout the day, beating myself up about the way I focused and seemed to harbour those feelings. Anything good vanished in a blur the moment anything labelled "bad" happened. This meant I felt that I lived a dull and negative life.

All my joy, laughter, fun was nothing compared with my negative emotions. The more I learnt to observe the more I noticed the balance of positive and negative. I would say I am lucky that the good far outweighs the bad on most days, but I was lost to that fact until I started to observe. Like so many things in this book, the root of my connection to my observer lies in meditation.

GIVING MY LIFE MEANING

"Abundance" has become a buzzword over the last few years, with it becoming the goal of many, and the subject of many books and films. Abundance for me used to mean money, and money for me had always meant happiness.

I am not sure where this belief came from, I am also not sure it was mine, but it did mean that I had a very skewed view of abundance. Living an abundant life can mean so much to people, lots of close friends, an amazing family, joy, freedom, creative expression, a love of work, but for me it was all about the dollar and nothing else. But with that, came an impressive amount of guilt.

Here I was, trying to be a good person, who seemed to have the sole goal of earning as many bucks as I humanly could. Attempting to do it in a loving way but feeling guilty at every step for each cent I made, as I did not know why I deserved it more so than anyone else on this earth. Why was I the lucky one who deserved to be born into a middle-class family, with a good education, and a well-paid job? Why was I not one of the starving children we so often see on our TV screens advertising some charity?

We have massive wealth disparity on this planet, and whilst I am in no situation to preach, it is a topic that I feel we need to address as a global society. But I believe the answer does not lie in money. It lies in understanding, deep down in your bones, as to what abundance really is.

Abundance is being able to live your life in a state of gratitude for everything that you already have. Abundance is the joy of knowing that you are happy and content with everything just as it is. That in this moment, all is well.

When you truly know you are abundant, your bank balance doesn't matter.

Abundance allows each of us to be individuals. It is conceited and arrogant beyond measure to assume that just because I want something, that the other six billion plus people on this planet would want the same. Who am I to dictate what will make people happy? Just because I dream of travelling the world with my children does not mean everyone will. Abundance lets us choose the dreams and goals that are ours, uniquely. Abundance gives us the measure to know that we are living the life that we are put here to live.

Love and abundance are very similar; they are both rooted in the gratitude of the present moment in the fleeting beauty of what we have right here and now. You cannot live in love and not be in abundance, and you cannot be fully abundant, yet not live from love. The more love you have to give, the more abundant you are.

It was 4 am one morning when I started to understand this fully. I was lying in our spare bedroom, next to my eldest son, who was running a high temperature. He had not been well for the last 24 hours and was very clingy. As I lay there listening to him talk to me about his favourite Thomas & Friends (TM) characters, I suddenly understood how blessed I was. I was tired, I was suffering from the same fever, and yet I had never felt happier, more alive and so in love with the life I had. In that moment, when I could have so easily slipped into the negative and the headache that just would not quit, instead I transcended the moment into one of utter bliss.

Abundance is evident everywhere, every day, but it requires our attention and gratitude for it to really embed itself in our lives.

In the past, I have been someone who has always needed a comparison. How am I doing against others? Am I thinner, richer, more fun, more successful, more intelligent? I needed to gauge and judge my progression against some arbitrary person. Not only were my chosen targets of comparison usually wildly inappropriate, but I am not sure they ever motivated me to achieve what I wanted to achieve.

I would pour through gossip magazines ranking myself against those featured, either tearing myself to pieces about how badly I was stacking up or feeling smug that my life was better than some poor soul who was that week's target for the UK media.

I came across an article, in one of the healthier magazines I would waste my money on, that talked about how comparing yourself to anyone else was the biggest mistake you could make if you were trying to be happy and abundant. By comparing ourselves to someone else we are not defining the life we want to lead by our own criteria, but by someone else's and we will always, always, fall short. Like many things that happen to me, the message took a while to sink in, but when it did, I noticed that many of the ambitions I had were not actually what I really wanted to do but were what I thought successful people should do, based upon what I had read about others.

I was building a life, not on my terms, but on those of strangers.

The life I want to live is surprisingly simple in many ways. I want to be able to tuck my kids in at night and tell them I love them, I want to be able to travel the world, and I want to create and teach others. Bizarrely, I also want to walk. If I had the time or lived in a country where the weather was slightly more dependable, I would walk everywhere. I love to walk, it makes me feel free, it gives me space, and it connects me with the world around me. Given half a chance, I would walk around the world. Maybe one day when the kids are a little older, I will.

Abundance to me is being surrounded with those I love, having the freedom to explore new places and new cultures and the privilege to share with others what I have learnt. Yet there are times when something so simple seems so far away because we are so often constrained by what other people will think.

If comparing ourselves to others is akin to a prison, then fearing the judgement of others is the warden. We regulate our lives by playing it safe and small; never truly giving in to what brings us the most joy.

I recently took a leap of faith. Due to a rather nasty situation I was dealing with professionally, I decided to quit with no plans. Now, based on everything I have been led to believe and told to do, this was stupid at best, but I felt that it was the only way that I was going to be able to make the changes I needed to build the life I wanted to lead. I had to give myself space to hear myself.

I would not recommend this to everyone, and I still have no idea how this will turn out, but I have never felt so safe or so sure that the leap I have taken is the right one.

I would never have done this or had the trust in myself if I had continued to compare myself to others or care how they would judge me. I value the opinions of others, especially those who I cherish, but theirs (or anyone else's) judgement is not going to stop me from trusting myself, my intuition or my talents.

I am proud of myself for the faith and trust I have learnt to have in myself. I am proud of the work I have done to let go of my critical voice, the limiting beliefs, and baggage that I have carried around for most of my life. But I still knew there was a final step I needed to take.

• • •

Learning to love myself was a significant step on my journey to becoming the leader and person I wanted to be, but I was still struggling to trust openly and completely. I could logically trust those around me who had, by my standards, not let me down. But my unconditional trust was hard to win and very easy to lose, and I would not tell you why.

My lack of trust in others was also stopping me from connecting and loving people completely, even my sons. I wanted to change that, but no matter what I did, I could not seem to understand what I needed to do or let go of.

But the universe always gives you what you need.

Walking into a lounge in a hotel in Bangkok, I met someone who turned my idea of trust on its head, and made me realise what genuine trust feels like.

I don't think either of us was expecting it, I certainly wasn't, but against all logic, I met someone who I trusted with every cell in my body immediately. And it scared the crap out of me!

Against my better judgement, my head and heart started battling once again.

I was struggling with how someone could make me feel safe and supported, and I pushed back. The feelings were so unfamiliar that my head refused to believe they were real and came up with every potential reason why they were false and should not be trusted. (There's that "should" word again!)

As I stepped back and started to examine how I was feeling, I wondered if it was possible to be as open with some others in my life who my head thought logical to trust and I started to see how little I shared of myself. I was not willing to open up and share what was going on in my heart to anyone, but I decided to give it a try.

I found that I was very comfortable to talk about what I had done but could not share how it made me feel. I was happy with facts and actions, but emotional responses left me mute. I was scared that others would use it against me, as a way to hurt me. I felt that I was arming the enemy, even though these were people I loved. My fear was visceral, and I literally felt that I was under attack each time I opened up, even just a little.

I knew so much about others but there was no-one in my life who I could, hand on heart, really say knew me. I had never let anyone get that close.

But I persevered. I am still not sure why, but the trust I was starting to acknowledge and accept in another was forcing me to address my relationships and friendships across the board. I admitted things that humiliated me. I talked about hopes of mine that I had previously kept to myself. Whilst I am not sure that everyone understood, they listened, and they didn't throw it back in my face as I had feared.

My head raced to search for evidence that trusting people was unwise: Were they talking behind my back? Who was sharing my confidences? I was looking everywhere I could to find a way to let myself retreat again into the seeming safety of my own little world.

Trust is not logical. It is an emotion allowing you to be vulnerable. It enables you to make the choice to open up to another and connect at a level I had never experienced before. It also gives you so much strength. But taking that leap, took more courage than anything else I had done previously.

I was sitting at a table under the stars in the French Alps, talking to two of the most important women in my life, when I suddenly noticed that I felt immense power in revealing my deepest fears. The safety of truly trusting another with your biggest fears was so completely opposite to what I was expecting. It was the realisation that by being completely open, completely me, there was support and others willing to help me solve my problems or achieve my dreams. For once I was not alone.

Starting to let people in and get close to my biggest hopes and fears was the part of the puzzle I was missing. It was the step that allowed me to fully connect and feel comfortable, not only with myself, but with others, as well. It was the missing ingredient to me becoming the leader I wanted to be.

It did not matter how much I loved myself if I could not open myself up to another, be vulnerable and trust. As strength does not just come from your belief in yourself, it is magnified and fortified by your faith in others and their faith in you. Once you truly believe how you are loved and seen through another's eyes, you can start to see what you can truly be and what you can accomplish. I had to learn to be loved.

But I was still scared of being loved and being vulnerable. I was scared of opening myself up to being hurt again, of people leaving me, of the sometimes-transient nature of love and learning that is life itself. Receiving love to me was still a lesson I needed to learn. I could love so deeply that it made me cry, but the thought of someone loving me like that seemed laughable. I could not believe that someone would be capable of loving me. It was then that the penny dropped that the final test of truly loving myself was letting another love me. I had to be vulnerable, I had to risk being hurt.

I knew I needed to dig into what was holding me back, what were the limiting beliefs that we stopping me from receiving love? I started documenting all the things that I would do for others, from the smallest activities such as sending a text just to check in, through to the larger time sacrifices, such as picking someone up from the airport at the crack of dawn. I was listing all the ways that I demonstrated love to those around me. The next step was to ask myself if I thought people would do these things for me, and even if I would have the courage to ask for it. I found it interesting that the disparity was so complete. I would do whatever was asked, not always with a smile, but I would do it. But I would not "bother" another. I did not feel worthy enough to ask for someone to sacrifice their time or energy on me.

I then widened my view to include my work life and I saw the same pattern as a leader. I would serve my team completely but fail to ask for the support that I needed. I was scared to be vulnerable to show the weaknesses I had. Instead of just seeing myself as human, I was desperately attempting to be super-woman.

• • •

My belief system has always been pretty fluid. I am well read in all manners of different philosophies and religions but have never firmly landed anywhere. But one tenet of my faith that has been consistent, is my belief that energy is the uniting force that binds us all. I call it my "Lion King" belief, the circle of life. What I realised was that, for me, the energy was all flowing out. My lack of willingness to open up and be fully vulnerable and open to anyone, completely blocked my ability to receive the love and support that I needed to continue to love others. I was a battery that was always going to burn out as I never recharged.

From the list of actions I had formulated, I sat down and started interrogating myself about why I believed others would not act the same way for me. What were the limiting beliefs I was holding on to that were stopping me from being truly vulnerable?

The list boiled down quite quickly to three:

- I am not worthy of love;

- People who love me always leave me;

- I don't deserve to be loved.

• • •

One of the lessons I had learnt through my journey to learn to love myself was that my beliefs and thought patterns were not unique. I started asking my friends and family if they held similar views of themselves, and was unsurprised but still saddened to discover, that most did. Nearly everyone I spoke to felt that they did not deserve to be loved in the way that they were willing to love another. Nearly everyone's fear of being vulnerable was down to the belief that somehow this openness would be used against them by others.

Later in this book, I describe the techniques I used to get to the bottom of these beliefs and reverse them into something that allows me to be open and vulnerable, but it is a constant process. "Vulnerability" is a buzzword at the moment, but it requires constant vigilance to maintain. Whilst our fight or flight response is no longer needed to protect us from a Sabre-toothed tiger, the same response is triggered when we undergo emotional pain and we instinctively try not to put ourselves in the same scenario again.

Each time an interaction doesn't go as you hoped or dreamed, each time someone doesn't act the way you expected, or each time you open yourself up to someone who is not ready to do the same, you risk the chance of getting hurt. Our instinct is to retract and build the walls up to protect ourselves again.

Vulnerability is not for the faint hearted, as it requires you to risk pain, again and again, in the hope that you can build deep connections with others that are unique and special. Vulnerability is the willingness to be loved as strongly and as deeply as you love.

The courage to write this book has not come from me purely facing my fears or bloody-mindedness. It has come from the unwavering knowledge that no matter what, I am blessed to have people in my life who believe in me. But these are not people who let me off easily either and that is half the joy of having them in my life. They know what I am capable of, so they don't let me wimp out and play small. They tell me what they truly think, good or bad, knowing that we are safe with each other to not hold back. The biggest kicks up the backside I have received, have often come from those I love, and who I allow to love me.

I am grateful for them every day, and I hope that no matter how far apart we all are, that they know what they mean to me, and know the strength they give to me to be a better person each and every day.

LEARNING TO LOVE MYSELF

Part of writing this book was to see if I could distil the journey that I have been on, and the mission that I want to achieve, into something teachable and actionable.

I wanted to see if the steps I had gone through were linked and sequential, if they could add value to others, and support them if needed. As the words began to come together, I started to see some definite themes or lessons, and a few definitive steps emerged. The rest of this book aims to lay out these steps and lessons in a way that I hope you find helpful and engaging:

- **Step 1** - You have to love yourself before you can lead with love. You don't need to be a saint or have no issues whatsoever, but you do need to be fundamentally OK with who you are and know your worth.
  * A great leader cannot be swayed by how they are judged by others * This step means different things for everyone and also seems to take the longest - it certainly did for me. But once I had started on the road to self-acceptance, it became clear what my role was in this life;

- **Step 2** - You have to model your behaviour around love and you have to practice what you preach, which means you need to accept that you are not perfect, but understand that you never stop learning and developing;

- **Step 3** - Prepare to be dealing with fear, a lot. Leading with love requires bravery and commitment, which means pushing yourself out of your comfort zone all of the time.

The lessons that emerged, seemed to be linked to each of the steps as I worked my way through them, and there appeared to be a distinct flow and sequence to what I had to learn to get to where I wanted to go. I have told these lessons as I have learnt them - some may resonate with you, others may seem so bleeding obvious that you might deem them useless, but each one was critical for me.

The lessons:

- Connect and listen to your heart;

- Let go of control and stress;

- Know your boundaries and what you stand for;

- Stop trying to please people;

- Open up to others;

- Be right here, right now.

• • •

Have you ever thought about how you love someone or even yourself? What is love and how do you express it or measure it? Have you ever thought about how to translate the feelings of love you have into actions of love? Conversely, have you ever thought about how you can translate actions of love into real feelings of love?

Love can be a soft caress or a tight hug, it can be a timely email or phone call, or a love shared between two strangers on a train. Love is whenever two humans let their souls connect for the briefest moment or for a lifetime.

Love comes naturally to us. Very few of us actually know the mechanics of loving; we just know how to do it. But as we grow up and adopt the beliefs of our parents, friends and societies, we lose the natural ability to love everyone, unconditionally. We decide that we will only love those who are worthy, who are in the same league, or who have something to offer us.

When I started to look at how I brought love into every aspect of my life, and especially in the workplace, I had to really force myself into loving those around me. I know we are designed to be loving beings, but it is so easy for our conscious and unconscious biases and prejudices to get in the way of our natural state. I had to re-learn how to love. I had to figure out and teach myself what is natural to us all, to those we instinctively care for. I had to create a framework for love. This may seem absurd, but having detached from my emotions for so long and spending nearly two decades in large corporate cultures, love was no longer natural for me. Even the concept of truly loving myself seemed alien.

Over years of observation and conversation, I have concluded that many of us have unlearnt how to truly love outside what is expected, so for most, that just means the family environment. We rarely treat strangers with respect, let alone love, and like any skill, we need to practice becoming good at it again.

I still do this little game where I choose someone, usually a complete stranger, but sometimes it can be someone I am struggling with, and I either picture them in my mind or look at them discreetly, and repeat to myself "I love you, I love you, I love you". Over and over I repeat this until I can feel my heart expand enough for a genuine feeling of affection to arise. Loving someone doesn't mean you have to love everything they do or stand for. It is about seeing past the veneer they want you to see, looking into their heart and soul, and knowing that they are also a pure being of love who also want only to love and be loved. It is about compassion, without judgement, that lets you see the purity of who they are beneath their ego.

I have created the process below over many years of trial and error, using many different techniques and sources. I am collecting more and more scientific data to back up my process and this will be continuously added to my website, but I do know it works. I use aspects of it every day and the process lets me work through the hard times and bring more joy to the good times. I have used the process with others to help them become better and to strengthen my teams.

There is one practice that over-arches the entire process, and that is presence - being in the moment, living in the now. I have spoken about this earlier, and I will dedicate a whole chapter to this life-changing habit later on.

But first, I learnt how to love myself. It is an ongoing process that I know will never stop and one that now feels like a joy rather than the chore it used to. Again, the steps and tools listed in the next few chapters may not be needed by everyone, but it is what I went through to get to the point where I am now, and I am continuing to learn how to be a better leader enabling me to coach my teams towards reaching their potential.

THINK IN INK

There is an excellent quote by Louise Hay which has become a bit of a mantra of mine. "You have to see the dirt before you can clean it up!"

For a number of years, I thought I could plough through any difficult situation or issue I had with the power of positive thought alone. Whilst this is definitely a step in the right direction, chanting "all is well" under your breath constantly won't make much difference and will get you a number of strange looks. You need to see, acknowledge, and then do something about the issues, circumstances, or people who are holding you back.

My first step in anything I now encounter is to sit and figure out what is bugging me. It is not always as easy as you immediately think, quite often anger is masking a sense of injustice or fear. For me, procrastination or distraction is nearly always fear. I will know that I want to do something and then I will find a million excuses why I can't do it now.

Our brains and our egos are experts at helping hide the root cause of many of our fears and blockages. Quite often we have become masters of self-sabotage, in an attempt to protect ourselves from feeling emotional pain. No one wants to deal with the bad stuff willingly, but that is life, so we need to come up with ways that allow us to do this efficiently and healthily.

I used to stew on issues that I encountered during the day, sometimes to the point where it would make it tough to fall asleep at night, until I started journaling. Having been a teenage girl with an obsessive love for stationery, I had spent quite a number of years writing down my thoughts, in multiple coloured inks, about boy bands, actors from Neighbours, or my latest crush, but I quickly dropped the practice of journaling as I got to university, because I thought it was childish.

I didn't understand the power of writing things down. There is something that unconsciously happens the moment I pick up a pen; it is like all the things I can't find a voice to say, feel safe being written down. The act of writing seems to remove blocks of communication for me, and the more I get my thoughts on paper, and it is old school paper, the more I can start to see clarity and connections between what has happened and what I am feeling. I can start to peel the layers of anger or frustration away and see the fear that lies beneath the surface. I can reach a point of understanding or acceptance for an incident that has happened through the day and let it go.

I now write every evening, sometimes just for a couple of minutes, other days I can write essays, but each time I learn something. Not necessarily right there, but that is the beauty of journaling, you can revisit what you have written days or even months later, and see what you need to learn very clearly in your own script.

My diaries are sacred to me, and the inner teenager in me would cringe if anyone were to read them, as they are my dirt. They are every thought that has gone through my head or heart that I am not ready to share and may never be willing to share. They are my fears, my failings, all written on a page for anyone to pick up and read, but the value I get out of the process, far outweighs the risk of anyone actually reading them.

I have diaries going back years around the house that one day I may be ready to let go of, but I know they still have something to teach me or remind me of. They are also a great aide memoir of how much I have grown and the person I have become.

The power of thinking in ink is incredible and is always my first step to figuring out which issue I need to deal with next. I love myself - it has taken years, but I do. However, it is also true that I am still going to have to continue to face issues I am carrying or aspects of myself that I don't like. So, I carry on writing.

• • •

The obstacle that blocks us from unconditionally loving everyone on this planet, nine times out of 10, is ourselves. Michael

Jackson (irrespective of what you think of him) said it beautifully, "If you wanna make the world a better place, take a look at yourself, and then make a change." The things that frustrate us in others are the things that consciously or subconsciously annoy us in ourselves. For example, the driver who cut me up in a rush on the way to dropping the kids at nursery, really annoyed me because I was frustrated with myself for not having got up before the boys, so again, the morning was a rush. Yes, the driver cut me up, but so what, my angry response had less to do with him, but it gave me an excuse to lash out at someone else, instead of looking at what I need to do differently.

The more we examine our triggers, the more we will learn about ourselves. I used to be really intolerant of incompetence; it used to bug me that people didn't know how to do things or do them well. After quite a significant amount of denial and deep digging into myself, I realised that I did not like my habit of "winging it". It scared me, and I felt that at some point I was going to get "found out". I subconsciously knew I was skating on thin ice and when I saw it in others, it really got my back up. I also knew that the fear of being found out was holding me back. I had to change my ways. I slowed down, I started preparing and learning, and quickly, I became incredibly tolerant of those who, before, I had classed as incompetent. I gained patience and a love of guiding others to learn. I started listening to my fear, not to stop myself but to understand myself more. Please do not let your fear lead you, but learn to listen to it, as it can teach you quite a few lessons about your behaviour. Once you have listened, tell it to get gone, then go and be the best, most courageous person you can be.

There is a theory that our external experience is a reflection of our internal attitude. I think there is a lot of truth in that. If you smile at others, you get smiles back. We have to get into the right headspace internally if we want to change our external world. That is why I spend quite a bit of time looking at myself, my behaviours, and those of the people around me.

Once you have figured out what is the root cause of the things that are bugging you, how do you then look at the changes you need to make to yourself to create the life you want to lead? Learning to love myself started with identifying my dirt, taking a long hard look at myself and becoming willing to accept that this is who I was.

Acceptance can be tough if there are aspects about yourself you don't like. It is really tough to allow yourself to accept them, for me, it felt like giving up the fight, but acceptance does not stop change. But change will not happen without acceptance.

Change will not happen without acceptance of what is.

Many ancient and modern teachings talk about surrender. I struggled with this concept until I started to look at it in a different way. An old boss of mine always used to tell me to pick my battles. He was frustratingly right because I wanted everything to be right all of the time and I felt that I needed to fix things if others weren't doing so. I could not accept things as they were, even if they were entirely out of my control or remit. This was most stark at work but equally applicable at home.

But this is what surrendering is; it is accepting that there are outcomes or situations that we cannot control. In fact, we are never in control of the outcome. It is accepting that whilst we will always do and be our best, sometimes we need not to fight the battle. This is not about quitting; it is using our abilities and energy in the right way. Making sure we are giving the best of ourselves and the most value. Picking my battles also means choosing which ones to let go of.

• • •

The major battle I had to decide not to fight was my war on being perfect. The concept of imperfection was utterly unacceptable to me. But what is perfect? It is not only an unattainable goal, but it is entirely unmeasurable. Ask anyone to give you metrics on perfection, and they will all be different. But I was determined to be perfect, and if I wasn't, I used to battle myself. What I realised was that I was not willing to accept myself as I was. I was unacceptable and therefore needed to be changed and fixed, but you cannot change what you cannot accept, so I lost over and over again - getting more and more frustrated with myself every time.

I was working through my issues, identifying new ones regularly, but I couldn't let go of the need to be perfect. I could not accept who I was, as I was. I could not learn to surrender. Alongside my journaling every night, I start categorising situations or outcomes that were bugging me, or issues I was trying to fix, into two areas; I can do something about this or this is completely out of my control. Once I had defined which category something sat in, I then wrote a list of actions I could do to remedy the situation, or a meditation or tapping routine to let it go.

The more I pulled these lists together, the more I realised how much was outside my control and that it was my desire to be in control of everything that was making me exhausted, and unable to surrender and accept. I needed to find a way to loosen my grip or I was going to burn myself out. Meditation was only doing so much. It was keeping me connected with my emotions, but I couldn't find a way to release and let them go through meditation. I started looking for ways to help me move forward and get rid of my baggage.

RUNNING INTO WALLS

You may now have a good idea of all the things that are currently bugging you about yourself. What next? Well, you need to recognise them, deal with them, and send them packing! There are hundreds of different ways to do this, so I am going highlight my favourite three, and also point you in the direction of how to learn much more about each of them.

A. Tapping (EFT)

I first came across Tapping (or Emotional Freedom Technique - EFT) about ten years ago and thought it was the most insane and crazy thing you can do. You literally tap parts of your body whilst saying really negative things about yourself. Nuts! I dismissed it as yet another weird fad that would go away. It was about three years ago when I came across it again and since my first encounter over a decade ago, the body of science to support its effectiveness had grown as had my tolerance for the slightly wackier (you should see my crystal collection!)

As the name suggests, tapping requires you to tap on a number of specific acupressure points across the body while focusing on any negative emotions or beliefs that you might be feeling at that time. To use the example of being cut up by another driver on your way to work, you would tap on these points whilst focusing on the frustration you felt at being cut up. After a few rounds, you miraculously feel the emotion evaporate. I often feel a wave of relief that still astounds me. I know it sounds completely nuts, but go check out The Tapping Solution (www.thetappingsolution.com) for some beginner videos and free meditations to give it a go. Nick and Jessica Ortner who run these programmes, are great at taking you through the process, and Jessica always seems to know exactly how to push the buttons I need to push on that day with one of her meditations.

The speed of the results I have had with tapping, makes it a tool that I think everyone should have in their arsenal, but it does require you to suspend your disbelief for a moment. As with most things, doing the work is the only way to really understand the miraculous power this therapy has.

Tapping is a tool I use daily to process anything negative I had felt during the day or to deal with an issue that has come up. To quote Shrek "Onions have layers. Ogres have layers." We all have layers, and as we get more and more into understanding ourselves and our triggers, you need to deal with each layer at a time, so I use tapping to allow me to do just that. It is rare that one session of tapping will completely clear a deeply rooted issue, but it will clear the trigger or response to that issue.

For example, it has taken many months for me to completely clear my fear of abandonment that was created when my father left, but each session I was able to remove the negative responses and behaviours I had due to that fear. The fear was so intertwined with who I was and how I acted, that I had to undo it one piece at a time. But once I had, it was gone completely.

The key to eradicating an issue completely is to focus on the feeling of what you are experiencing, instead of the words you are saying. Feel your way through the process and trust it. But you also need to be willing to be free of your issues. I have used so much of my baggage as an excuse for not doing things that these excuses have become like security blankets; things that make me feel safe but are potentially doing more harm than good. It is only when you are willing to let go of these supports that you can fully clear yourself of the fears and limiting beliefs that are holding you back.

No one lives a perfect and utterly carefree life, but tapping allows me to balance the good and the bad of each day, dissolve stress, and every so often, deal with a significant issue that may arise that I am now ready to face and release.

So how do you do it? As mentioned above there are some great videos on The Tapping Solutions site which I highly recommend, but if you are dying to give it a go now, I will give you a brief beginner's guide to tapping in my own words. Please note that I am not trained in tapping, but I am an avid user.

There are two main aspects of tapping that allow you to move through your negative emotions and release them. First are the actual tapping points. There are eight across your body (I have created what I hope is a handy graphic below). Start on your hand, at what is known as the Karate Chop point. It is the fleshy spot, on the outer side of your hand, at the bottom of your little finger. The Karate Chop point is the first point in the sequence.

Karate Chop Point

You then move to five points on your face. The eyebrow point is at the point where your eyebrow starts near the centre of your forehead. Second, is the side of the eye. This is not the temple, but the bone by the side of your eye socket. Thirdly, under the eye. This is, again, on the bone just under your eye, below your pupil.

Next, is under your nose between your nostrils and your top lip. The last point on your face is under your bottom lip, halfway between your lip and your chin, just in the natural fold most of us have there.

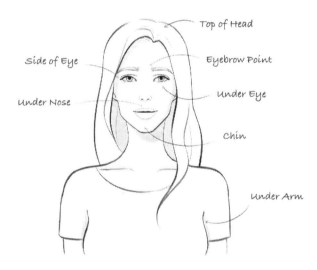

Top of Head

Side of Eye

Eyebrow Point

Under Nose

Under Eye

Chin

Under Arm

The sixth point is called the collar bone point but, it is not actually on your collar bone. Find where your collar bones join by your throat and then follow your collar bone out, about an inch towards your shoulder, then drop an inch below that. That is your collar bone point. You can tap on either side.

The seventh point is called under your arm, and it can be found about a hand's width under your armpit. The final point is on the top of your head, right in the centre.

As I mentioned, you can tap on either side of your body depending on what is most comfortable for you. Or, as I do, tap both sides at once.

These tapping points are crucial to the process, but they are only one half of it. The second half is being able to connect in with the negative emotion that is troubling you; seeing and speaking your dirt. Sometimes this is very acute, especially in the case of something happening to you in the present or the recent past, but for many of us, we are trying to clear issues that go back decades, and it can be harder to access the emotion itself.

In order to help you tap (get it!) into that emotion, we start by vocalising the issue at hand and noticing in your body what reaction you may have. Is there a tightening in your stomach or throat? Does your heart feel as though it has a tight grip around it when you recall a memory or talk about a particular individual? Notice what your body is trying to tell you.

Vocalising any issues you may have allows your body to respond, and once you have a response you can gauge the level of your pain or discomfort on a scale of zero to 10. 10 being extreme discomfort or pain, zero being not an issue at all.

Once you have a number, you can start tapping and talking through the issue. When I first started tapping, I realised I talked a lot, but I did not feel anything. Now, the amazing thing with tapping is that it still works, but where you make huge break-throughs is when you can feel the emotion in the moment you are both tapping and talking it through. The way I think about it is that I have to give my feelings a voice and sometimes they have some strange and tough things to say.

I am going to give you an example that was a very real issue for me that I used tapping to turn around completely.

I hated myself, quite viscerally. I would put on my confident face, but inside I hated everything that I was. I thought I was what my grandmother told me: fat, boring and ugly. I also truly believed that I was useless, so I hated myself for that as well. My hatred of me was not limited to the physical; it was emotional and intellectual, as well.

When you start tapping, you initially begin on the Karate Chop point and whilst you are tapping here, you say a statement that sums up the issue you are trying to deal with and that also acknowledges where you are. In this example I would have said:

"Even though I hate myself so much and everything that I am and do, I can feel this in my body, as my stomach tightens and my throat closes at the mere thought of liking myself. I acknowledge how I feel and it is ok."

There are lots of different ways that I have seen these initial statements crafted and there are hundreds of free tapping scripts online if you don't know where to start, but just by vocalising where you are and how you feel starts the process of healing.

You say this statement whilst tapping on the karate chop point three times. I don't know the reasoning why you say it thrice, but I often find that this repetition allows you to tune into your body and start to really feel where you are holding onto any tension or negative emotion. I also find that I tend to have more to add to the statement by the third time and I am really giving my dirt a voice.

When I started tapping, I found it hard to accept that I was trying to engage, and sometimes enhance negatives feelings. It felt wrong to focus on the negative and sometimes, it still does, but you need to acknowledge and accept the negative before you can transform it into positive and let it go. I have likened this to an addiction; you have to firstly acknowledge you have a problem before you can deal with it. Negative beliefs and emotions are very much the same.

Once you have voiced your initial statement three times, whilst tapping on your Karate Chop point, you then move through the other points: eyebrow, side of eye, under eye, under nose, under mouth, collar bone, underarm, and top of head; in that order, whilst saying whatever comes up for you.

When you start, scripts can be very helpful, but there is no set formula for what you have to say. Just say what you feel is right, not what you think is right. As you move through the sequence of eyebrow through to the top of the head, over and over, you will start to feel the intensity of the emotional change. Sometimes, it will get more intense before it subsides and there are times when I burst into tears. Just let it happen, but don't stop tapping.

When I have spoken to friends about tapping they often have the same questions. How hard do you have to tap? How long does it take? How do you know it's working? Are you nuts?

You just tap. You are not hitting yourself hard, you don't need to pound parts of your body - just gently tap each point. I tend to use two fingers and I quite often tap on both sides of my body at the same time, but you don't have to. Do what feels right for you.

It takes as long as it takes. Sometimes I can clear a small stress or issue in a couple of minutes, and there are other times when I am there twenty minutes later, sobbing my heart out and still tapping, but every time the issue lessens significantly. There may be times that I have to revisit an issue. For example, my self-hatred took months to get to the bottom of and release, but eventually, it did go.

I know when tapping is working because my measure of intensity reduces. I write down in my journal each statement that I am working on, as this gives me the chance to track my progress. Most days I can see issues disappear, but I can then also revisit deep-seated issues and beliefs on a regular basis, to ensure that I am really getting to the root of the issue and letting it go.

Tapping has also let me see that I have not only held onto issues that are holding me back, but I have actively put in blocks or resistance to letting them go, as I have started to treat these issues as protection, stopping me from progessing in my life. As I mentioned, these have become security blankets for me, life seemed safer with them. So, alongside tapping through the issues that are coming up, I now always ask myself the following three questions when I am tapping:

1. Do I have any resistance, anywhere in my body, to letting this issue go?

2. Do I have any blocks, conscious or unconscious, in any part of my body, to letting this issue go?

3. Do I have any fear of letting this issue go in any cell in my body?

I let my intuition give me the answer, and if I do find any resistance, blocks or fear, I tap and ask that they may be given a voice so that they can be heard and that I can then let it go. I have found that by using these three questions, I can get to the root of more issues faster and clear them more effectively. It may take a little longer but this works best for me. Play around with what feels right for you and change the wording as you need to.

I may be nuts, but this works. Give it a go! The more I clear my limiting beliefs, issues and day to day stresses, the more open I am to other people, and the more I can support and love them. As a leadership tool, it has helped me stay calm in times of significant stress, get over any fear of networking or public speaking, and have the courage to become genuinely vulnerable to those I lead and work with.

Unlike any other tool I use, including meditation, tapping is so easy that it can be done anywhere, and I have on a regular occasion disappeared to a quiet spot, or even the restroom, before a big presentation or announcement, to calm my stress or anxiety with tapping. I also use it before I meditate to clear anything that is playing on my mind so that I can fully relax into my meditations.

B. Gratitude

If this is not your first foray into the world of the spiritual, self-help or love leadership, you will have heard about the power of gratitude. If you haven't, then listen up as this is going to change your life. Gratitude is the fastest way to build a force-field of love. Corny, I know, but the more grateful you are for every great thing, person and situation in your life, the harder it is for you to be negative.

I have a small ceremony that I do with my kids every night. They don't understand it, and they rarely give me an answer, but after I have tucked them into bed and told them to dream big, I ask them to them to tell me what made them happy that day. Whilst they lie there warm, snug, and potentially thinking they have been born into a madhouse, I list off the top five things I am grateful for that day. It can be as simple as having a warm home to come back to on a cold winter's night, all the way through to pure wonder at the magnificence of this world. Whatever it is, I know that by the time I have finished my little mental list, I will leave the boys' rooms filled with such gratitude for having had another day on this planet. It also helps me deal with some of the small day to day frustrations of parenting two boys under the age of four, as it acts as a daily reminder of the joy they bring to me.

Gratitude is powerful; so powerful, in fact, that just this practice alone can transform your life completely. Again, the power comes from feeling the gratitude for everything on your list, not just writing or speaking the list outloud. If this doesn't work to begin with, write your list of the top five to 10 things you are grateful for. Then close your eyes and start to feel how you would feel if even one of those things weren't true. How would you feel if you didn't have a warm home to come back to on a cold winter's night? Pretty terrified and lost would be my answer.

At the beginning of my journey, it was much easier for me to engage with my gratitude for life by initially feeling the negative emotion I would have if this were not true. So give it a go. How would you feel if one of the items on your list was not true? Start to feel it, then feel the relief and the gratitude start to grow, and appreciate that, for you, the opposite is the reality. Over time, it will become much easier for you to start to feel the warm glow of gratitude immediately, so don't worry, you won't be focussing on the negative for long, it is just a way to start you feeling something. If too much negative does come up, then tapping is a great way to release the negative emotions and move into the positive.

Now, at some point every day, I sit down and write my gratitude list, and I spend time thinking of all the wonderful things in my life - all the great events that happened during the day - it always grounds me, brings me back to feeling fantastic, and excites me about the life that I lead.

• • •

Gratitude is simple but powerful. I have found that I used to confuse hard with complex and easy with simple. By this, I mean I would procrastinate about doing a task or adopting a habit as I thought it would be too hard, and in my head, I would equate that to complexity. I would claim I didn't know how to start, or did not have enough knowledge to start, the problem was too difficult to solve, but actually, I was shying away from the effort required. For me, this was based in a belief that I wasn't worth making the effort for. I confused complexity with hard as I was not willing to value myself. I also mistook rituals, like this one around gratitude, as easy.

Gratitude is not easy; it requires thought and connection. It requires you being present enough throughout your day to notice the things that make you smile. It takes time to sense the feeling of the sun on your skin or to stop and smell the roses in full bloom. That, again, requires effort, but it is simple. Simple and easy are not the same, one still requires effort but can deliver so much value. Don't underestimate the power of a simple task or ritual.

Making an effort to build a habit around gratitude is worth it. I also found that the simple act itself starts to make me more grateful for myself and, thus, created a virtuous circle, where I was gaining from this new habit on every level. Many of the things in our lives that we believe are holding us back are not complex, but they may be hard, and the question we need to ask ourselves is; "Am I worth the effort?"

There is one additional point I would like to make about gratitude. Whilst it is so vital that we are grateful for what we have right here, right now, it doesn't stop you from dreaming of being bigger and better. For a few years, I have had a dream of leading the world to love. It may sound very lofty and self-important, but I have had weeks where I have had the same dream over and over again, and this longing in my heart to change how we are in this world. To be honest, I have never known how I will achieve such heights, and I still don't know every step, but gratitude has allowed me to feel the strength and the joy to know that I have everything right here, in this very moment, to take the next step on the path to my dream. Gratitude helps drive me towards my goals, and it is with the power of gratitude that I hope one day I will achieve what I dream of doing.

So never confuse gratitude with complacency. Gratitude is not about giving up and stopping where you are now, but it is about acknowledging the wonder and joy of everything that you currently have. Even if it may not seem like very much at this time, all of us have something to be grateful for. It may be as simple as a roof over our heads, or drinkable water from the tap, but these simple things are far more than many have.

So, each day before you go to sleep, create your list of the things you are grateful for and then drift off to dream of angels and adventures.

C. Create Your Mantras

Most of us have beliefs that, if we were to examine them in any detail, would have us laughing in the aisles. We have picked these up through our childhood, and subconsciously, embedded them into our everyday behaviours. Most of us now find it amusing that the majority of this world once thought that the earth was flat, but we all seem quite happy to hold beliefs about ourselves that are equally inane. Just take my example of believing I was useless. Factually, this is entirely incorrect, if I was actually useless I could do nothing, and for a person who has managed to survive four decades on this planet and hold down a steady job for at least two of those, letting go of this incorrect belief should be simple. But it takes some effort.

The technique of logically investigating each belief is, for me, the slowest method I have used, but when I was so led by my head and not willing to tap my way through issues for fear of looking like a numpty, it worked.

Sit down, take out a notebook and start writing down all the things that you believe about yourself. As I said, many of these beliefs have been taken on board subconsciously so it will take some time before you can uncover all the crazy beliefs that are standing in your way of living your best life, so just start with the ones that come up first. Once you have written a number of negative beliefs about yourself, start gathering evidence to support that belief.

For example, a widespread belief is that "I am not good enough." Really? At what? What exactly are you not good enough at? When you start examining this belief most people find that they cannot quantify or qualify this belief. As adults, we need to take responsibility for our beliefs, and we must be able to look at nonsense for what it is. You don't believe you are good enough at being you? Who is, apart from you?

You are the only "you" the world will ever know. So the only person stopping you from being good enough is YOU. Are you really willing to sit there for the rest of your life and judge yourself? No-one else can measure or say what the best version of you is, apart from you. Write down all the things that make you good at being you.

Then choose three and write them out on some pieces of paper and stick them around the house, like on the fridge or the bathroom mirror. Put them in places that ensure you see them numerous times during the day and start repeating them to yourself over and over again.

One of my favourite tricks was to use an affirmation when climbing stairs. I used to work on the 9th floor and would quite often climb all the way up. If I used a mantra such as "I'm happy, healthy and wealthy" I would be sitting at my desk before I even noticed. However, without using a mantra, I was labouring up each flight wondering what the hell I was doing to myself and if a heart attack was imminent. The reason I love mantras or affirmations is that they serve two purposes: firstly, they give your mind something to play with instead of stressing out, and secondly, they make you feel awesome.

There is a point when your thought, repeated often enough, starts to elicit a feeling, and that is when the magic happens. Pick a mundane activity you do regularly and add a mantra.

• • •

In summary, write down all the crazy, stupid and downright dangerous beliefs you have about yourself and this world, and start turning them around into positive mantras that you can use to change your life. Use tapping to release the beliefs once and for all, and then build your mantras to change your life.

If you want to read more on how affirmations can bring significant change, then any book by Louise Hay is a great starting point. I will suggest a few in the resources section at the end of this book.

Committing to Bold Action

So, you have figured out what annoys you and raises your blood pressure, you have dug deep and realised that this is because of something you believe about yourself or the world, and you have begun to work through these issues by (hopefully) a combination of tapping, gratitude, writing down your beliefs and changing them into mantras. Now is the really tough part. You need to commit to changing.

Hey, didn't we cover that earlier? - "You quoted Michael Jackson and everything", I hear you ask? Well, it's part of it. But that was about self-awareness and acceptance. It is impossible to change something that you are not aware of. Until you know you have a habit, you cannot stop it.

Most people are actually good at identifying the habits, beliefs and qualities about themselves that aren't serving them. What they aren't so good at is then committing to letting them go and changing. Change takes commitment, and commitment in most people's minds means giving something up which they like - also known as a sacrifice.

It is at this point when people either give up on the path to joy and love, or step back and determine if the short-term "sacrifice" is worth the long-term gain. Or even, in some cases, if the short-term enjoyment is worth the long-term loss - think about eating that ice cream if you are trying to lose a few pounds.

Personally, I had never been good with commitment to the long-term; I would rather have the extra glass of wine or chocolate instead of the "pain" of getting up 30 minutes earlier to go to the gym. I had tended to embrace the ease of being a "busy fool" rather than work towards the things that will make the most significant difference.

It was one day when I was sitting in a park in Sheffield, having dropped my youngest son off at his first settling in session at nursery, that I had a moment of clarity. It was a beautiful, blue sky, May day; the sun was just starting to get some strength to it and all of a sudden it was like someone came up behind me and smacked me around the back of the head with a frozen halibut.

I had spent years working on myself, understanding all my triggers, trying to improve every area of my life by journaling and writing lists, but I was not actually willing to commit to doing anything about building the life I wanted. I had huge dreams about enabling and leading global change, but I was waiting for a miracle to happen as I was not willing to commit to the hard work it was going to take to get there.

I would dream of what I would do with a big lottery win, and how that would solve everything. But I was not seemingly willing to get off my butt and do anything differently.

I was using my baggage to weigh myself down into inaction. I would commit a couple of weeks to something and then give up claiming it never worked - whether it was a diet, a new productivity tool, or a better way to show up in the world. I never gave new habits time to form or have an impact. I wanted an overnight miracle or nothing at all. I wanted change NOW, but I was not willing to put in the hard work to change.

It is said that new habits on average take three months to embed themselves into our daily routine, that is a quarter of a year that we have to commit to, at least, for a new way of being to start taking root. So we need to let go of the old excuses and commit to action.

Love in action is a habit. When we were young, it came naturally, but we build ways of behaving to fit in and protect ourselves (or so we thought) so by the time we become adults, very few of us know how to live through love. It takes commitment each day to love a little harder, a little longer and a little deeper.

Are you willing to make a commitment? Are you willing to learn to love yourself a little bit more each day for the next 90 days? If the answer is yes, Hooray! If not, I want you to sit down and write down your dream life. Go wild! Write a life beyond your wildest dreams, write about all the things that you want to see, do and feel. Write as if money, time and love were no object. Once you have finished, read it through, twice. Are you really sure that you are not willing to commit just a little bit each day to get closer and closer to this dream?

I got stuck in another cycle, I knew I had to commit to action but I could not for the life of me figure out what that was. It took me nearly a year to actually equate committed action to creation. Sounds weird right? We spend a lot of our lives doing: we do the shop, we do the laundry, we do our hair, but we rarely create and that is where I was going wrong. I mentioned earlier that I had a tendency to be the "busy fool" and I was. I was foolish enough to believe that just getting on with doing stuff would bring about the changes I wanted to see in me, my life and the world around me.

The plain fact is, that doing is great, but creating is the key.

I have never considered myself creative. I am not artistic, musical or particularly good at the arts. I don't enjoy them much. I am one of those people who will charge through a museum at breakneck speed or yawn through an opera. I am not arty. And that is fine not everyone is, but I had missed the point of creation. Being able to create does not need you to have the skills of Picasso or Mozart, it requires you to have the guts to try.

I was someone who said they are not creative because I was filled with fear of being judged by others for what I created. I was someone who was scared to actually be myself and stand by what I enjoyed doing. I was scared to stand out. I was scared to try anything different. I was told at school that I could not write, so I stopped. I used to endlessly journal as a teenager, I loved it. I even considered writing a novel when I was 17, but I was told that I didn't have any talent, so instead of continuing what I enjoyed, I stopped. I was paralysed to create by the negative opinion, mainly of my teachers and of others, that I ceased to do many of the activities that actually filled me with joy.

I was scared of the judgement if people read my work and thought it was rubbish. I was scared of drawing (another thing I actually enjoy doing) in case I was criticised. I loved singing, but you would only find me doing that in the safety of the shower or my own kitchen. I stifled my creativity because I was scared of the opinion of others.

I justified this fear by drowning myself in my work, spending every spare minute grafting for someone else's advantage. I avoided the topic of hobbies, the closest I got was running, but that is hardly creative.

The problem was that my fear became pervasive. It seeped into every aspect of my life, and, over time, I ended up not being able to stand by anything I felt or disagreed with. Committing to action meant I had to commit to creating, commit to facing my fear of other people's judgement and start doing the things that made me smile for the long-term. The next time you hear yourself, or someone else, say that you are not creative, stop, question that belief and use one of the techniques above to identify the fear that is stopping you from bringing your creative force into this world, because this world needs your talent.

• • •

Having decided to write, I realised that I had to have a weekly target to commit to otherwise nothing would happen. I knew that given half a chance I would find excuse after excuse not to sit at the keyboard and write. I create a weekly target of 3,500 words (only 500 a day) to force myself into the habit of creating. Some days are easier than others, but every day I sit down and I write. Slowly, over time it has become a habit and it has become a release.

Just setting the commitment and sticking to it does not mean I am perfect, I have fallen off the writing wagon a number of times, and the excuses have surfaced to let myself off the commitment I have made ("I am tired" or "I don't have time" being two of my favourites.) But setting the commitment to myself, also forced me to question these excuses and commit to the act, even if they were true. I have, on so many occasions, sat down and written 500 words or more of complete nonsense only to delete them the following day, but I still did it. And that is all the matters.

Commit to change, set yourself goals that you can measure each week to ensure that you are progressing. Aim for progress, not perfection.

• • •

The final step is to learn to be bold. Take your dreams and expand them a hundred-fold. Take your love and make it boundless. Take your energy and give it freely. Don't hold yourself back to fit in. Take a leap and see where you will end up.

I cannot tell you the amount of time and energy I have wasted in my life conforming to what others think I should be. Changing myself to please others when it doesn't suit or serve me and my dreams. I don't want someone telling me how I can be better, that is down for me to decide. I am not here to please others, I am here to love them, to support them and to help them figure out for themselves who they want to be.

I used to avidly lap up feedback, adjusting my behaviour and my personality to fit what others, mainly my superiors, wanted me to be. Until one day I got given a piece of feedback that was so ridiculous and designed to make me second guess myself, where I realised all I was doing was endlessly trying to please people. I was not being my best me; I was once again trying to live up to other people's expectations. So I gave up on feedback. I am not saying that so I could become rude, complacent or not try my best, but it did mean that I started to take everything I heard with a pinch of salt. I started to think about why someone was giving me this feedback, rather than just accepting it on face value and changing myself because of it.

We spend so much time moulding ourselves to please others that we don't allow ourselves to be brave, bold, or to do the things we have always wanted to do.

There are so many social media posts and quotes about following your dreams and finding your passion, and we wistfully read them, longing to be brave enough to actually do anything about it. Well, that is not living. It is not taking hold of the gift we have been given and using it to its fullest. We are living a half-life if we are not brave enough to be bold.

Take time to understand the limits of your comfort zone and then endlessly push at the boundaries - make this into a daily game. I love that moment during the day when I feel my stomach tense because I know I have just got to that place. I am at the edge of my zone, and I am about to push myself over the line. It can be as simple as sharing how you really feel, with emotion, in the workplace. All the way through to deciding to write and publish a book on love. Trust me; that decision and the follow-through of actually writing, pushed my limits nearly every day. I had so many beliefs and rational arguments to why this book was a bad idea, but I came back to the same question every time. Am I saying that because I want to play safe or do I push on through because I want to be bold and follow my heart and my dreams?

I have always loved writing, but I had never had the courage to embrace my passion and create something of my own.

The thing that fascinated me the most was the amount of support I got from those around me when I spoke about (what I thought was) my slightly insane plan of writing a book. My partner told me one night how proud he was of me. My friends kept on asking me when it would be ready as they were keen to read it and my coach was working with me to build a promotional plan. I stepped outside my comfort zone and did not find the judgement or humiliation I expected. I found support, love and the fact that I was inspiring others to give their creative talent a go.

The number of people who have told me that they wished they could write a book has been surprising, and when asked what was in their way, the excuses have been endless. I think we are all creative beings and we long to be able to express ourselves. So, why not give it a go? I certainly encourage everyone to. You don't have to publish or show anyone your paintings, but you should push yourself to try.

It is about taking small steps, don't expect yourself to create a masterpiece overnight or release a best-selling album next week. Most of us don't know where our creativity will take us; I had never guessed a book! But it is by starting to build your creative muscle that your power will grow. This book actually started when I began journaling again. Just getting my thoughts down on paper about the day, what went well, what could have gone better and then one day, sat in a hotel bar in Hong Kong, this book started and before I knew what was happening, I had written 5,000 words, and I knew what I was committing to. Start small - you never know where you may end up.

Go on, do yourself a favour. Pick up a paintbrush or a note-pad and pen and give it a go. Go join a choir and sing your heart out or bake a cake for the office. Start boldly thinking of the creative activities that give you joy and go and have fun!

Real bravery always starts from the heart.

CONNECTING WITH YOUR HEART

When I first started wanting to live from my heart, I didn't know where to start. Emotions were something that I could not control or really gauge effectively, let alone learn from. I had taught myself from an early age that emotions were not something to be encouraged. I was embarrassed and terrified by them. The more I thought about my connection to my feelings, the more distant a concept they got, until I realised where I was going wrong. I was thinking about it!

I had to learn to feel my way through this, and that meant calming my mind enough to hear my heart. But the first step I had to learn was how to feel. Repressing your emotions over a period of time does not change the intensity of the emotion when you do come to feel it, but it does make you less likely to feel. You become numb or, more accurately, so disengaged from your emotions that you can look at them as an annoying fly at a picnic. Something that you may swat at occasionally, but you are not going to really bother to do much about it.

Removing years of repression, or suppression, and learning to feel again, took me a long time. I can remember someone telling me to get angry about the fact that my father had abandoned me, and I couldn't. I didn't know how to be angry. I could act it but to engage and feel the rage racing through my veins was alien to me. The same could be said of joy. Any emotion on either side of the spectrum left me drawing a blank.

I was travelling in Cambodia when my emotions first started to emerge, and I started to understand what it felt like to feel, what it meant to engage with another, in my case, it was prompted by a graphic insight into human suffering. I was in Phnom Penh visiting, what I can loosely describe as, a tourist attraction. The Tuol Sleng Genocide Museum is a reminder of the atrocities of the Khmer Rouge regime. The museum used to be a school, and as I walked from classroom to classroom learning of the torture and murder that happened to innocent victims, I felt more and more horrified by the depths that humans will stoop to protect their ideals and egos.

One of the rooms has a number of small brick cells where torture victims were held between "sessions" and on the walls are paintings done by previous inmates of the horrific acts they had to live through. The creation of these art pieces is meant to serve as both therapy to the survivors and a stark reminder to visitors of what happened within the walls of the prison. They were graphic, gut-wrenching and visceral. This was not art to please or entertain; this was art to heal, to release, to allow a soul to put everything they had on paper, so that they could finally let go of the horror they endured. Everything I saw on the walls hit me as a warning of what numbness and disconnection could cause a human to do. This was neighbours killing neighbours, torturing a childhood friend, children killing on demand, all because an elite few had decided to disconnect us from ourselves and each other.

Something clicked in me, the numbness lifted for a moment and I felt something. I now know it was compassion, but at the time, it was enough to feel a connection.

I stood there with tears rolling down my face, not purely for the poor souls that had suffered so much but also because I could not answer a very simple question. If I had lived through this time, which side would I have been on? I am well educated so I would have been a target. But I have always been able to act. Would I have been a torturer or one of the tortured? I was gripped by the terrifying realisation that in all likelihood, I would not have stood up against the regime. I would have submitted. I was so unsure of my own allegiances and values that I would have followed the herd. I may even have joined the oppressors to ensure my safety and quality of life.

I left the room and stepped into the sunshine of a courtyard. Children were now using this area to play an impromptu game of football. They were having fun and the sound of their laughter filled the air. At one end of the pitch was what looked like an over-sized goal post. I stepped down three steps and lent against the wall trying to pull myself together, trying to convince myself that I could never do what I had just seen, that I would stand up and fight. I looked up and in front of me was a photo of the very same goal posts with four bodies hanging from it. This innocent game of kick about was taking place underneath gallows. I was promptly sick.

As part of my motorbike tour of Phnom Penh, I was meant to be visiting the Killing Fields that afternoon. My driver was waiting for me as I staggered out of the prison. It was about 32 degrees Celsius, but I was freezing and shaking as I climbed onto the back of his bike. I had to see everything. I had to see the extent of what humans could do to each other. I had to understand, and I had to feel. We sped out of town and into the countryside. I felt the tears drying on my cheeks and the wind stinging my eyes. The whole journey was a blur as that question raced around my mind, "which side would I have been on?"

We came to a quiet and picturesque field, which felt vaguely like the English countryside on a warm summer's day. I dismounted and was pointed in the direction of a mound. The place was silent, eerily so, and there were only me and a couple of others there. I walked through a small line of trees and came across the monument that had been erected to commemorate everyone who was slaughtered. A pyramid of skulls that had been excavated from the site. The base of the pyramid was about four or five metres wide and reached up to well over six metres. I let my gaze move upwards meeting the empty stare of hundreds of human skulls. I was literally face-to-face with the victims and I still didn't know if I would have been one of them or part of the problem. I had no idea who I was or what I stood for.

That day shook me to my core. I remember returning to my guest house by the lake and staring into the distance, confused and concerned by what I had seen and what I had felt. I regret that it took me so long after that event to truly understand the impact it had and where it would take me, but we all have our journeys to go on and our lessons to learn.

That day I knew I was too young to know what to do with the knowledge I had learnt about myself, but ever since that day, each time I needed to learn about treating others, the images of that room, the goalposts and the seemingly endless tower of skulls come back to me in some form. They remind me of who I could become if I am not connected and deliberate about the person I want to be. They remind me of what I fear I would be capable of doing if I do not stand up for my values and live from love. They remind me to be better than I was that day.

It was some years before I learnt that these memories were prompting me to change. Whilst they were starkly there as reminders, I did not understand that they were asking me to make a choice. They were demanding that I connect with my heart and my feelings; they were demanding compassion and unconditional love for every human being. They were telling me that was the only way that we could avoid yet another genocide incident happening in our human history - be compassionate. Treat others how you want to be treated.

I needed to learn to connect to my heart on demand. I could not wait for events like this to force it to happen; I had to choose to sink my awareness into my chest and let that guide me through my life.

First, I needed to discover a way to start engaging and investigating my emotions. A method that would allow me to explore my feelings in a degree of safety, allowing me to learn and feel.

Meditation is truly magical, but it is not something that most of us can cultivate as a constant state. It is hard work and takes time, patience and a comfy cushion. But if I was going to lead with love, I needed a way that would allow me to use my heart as quickly and as effectively as I use my head.

To set some expectations, this took me a lot of time, practice, and willingness to slow down my decision making in the short-term. I was so used to just going with what my head said, that I knew that to be able to listen to my heart, I would have to be still, I had to give myself space to hear. I am not sure what it looked like from the outside, but against my standards, I became indecisive and vague, and I often got frustrated with myself.

The first step for me was to set up a daily meditation practice, even if it is just for three minutes, to connect with my breath. I allow myself to become still, feeling the air move in and out of my lungs, feel my chest rise and fall. I decided that I wanted to incorporate this into my everyday life as I knew I would struggle to "dedicate" time to this, so I used to do this at the bus stop, in between meetings or even on the toilet. I was just spending a few minutes each day checking in with my breath. If I got 15 to 20 minutes of meditation in every so often then that was amazing, but I knew for long-term success, I needed to build the habit and that takes time.

I also knew that I couldn't get this right without taking my brain with me, I knew I could not fight against my head and my thoughts. I needed to keep it occupied before it distracted me, so I started asking myself questions throughout the day - simple things like; "how am I breathing?", "Do I feel anything at this moment?" This practice aimed to get me learning, and forming a habit, checking in with my body, and using my breath was the easiest way to do this by far.

Once I got comfortable with checking in with my breath and my body, I decided to extend the time I took, just once a day, usually just before I went to sleep in order to settle down, close my eyes and as I started to notice my breath, I tried to see if I could sense my heart beating. Could I feel that rhythmic sensation in my chest? It often helped to physically touch my chest, resting my palm, or even a finger, on my sternum, which allowed me to more easily move my awareness to my heart. At this point, I needed to start learning something else as well: patience. It took me weeks to perfect this, but eventually, I was able to connect in and sense my heartbeat.

So now I could connect to my heart, how was I going to use this connection? I sat down and connected with my breath as I had done numerous times before, but I couldn't get focused. Every time I tried to reconnect with my heart to start feeling, my brain would kick in or my body would ache to the point of distraction. I seemed to be stopping myself from taking the next step. It was like I was running into a brick wall every time

I wanted to explore this connection with my heart further. And, in a way, I was.

Years of numbness had, metaphorically, built a wall around my heart of suppressed emotions and heartache. Unconsciously, I was terrified of going near this. My brain was logically telling me to sit longer, to breathe deeper, to ignore the pain in my body, but I was unconsciously protecting myself from feeling.

It also didn't help that I wanted to get this over and done with in just one session. Little did I know, I had a long way to go, in fact, peeling away the layers of emotions is most probably a lifetimes work as you never stop feeling, but time and consistency of practice have meant that I can now connect with my heart and use it to support and guide me. Connecting with how my heart feels changes. I am sitting here writing this after a long day in the office, and my heart has a number of sensations around it. I can feel the underlying joy of being me, alongside an anxiety that I am pushing myself too much at the moment, as well as a sense that I need to let go of some control. As I sink deeper into these feelings, I can sense that I know in every fibre of my being that all is well. Our heart is not there just to love us but also to teach us where we may need to refocus, let go or allow.

There are times when I sit down to sense how I really feel about a situation, and I am surprised by the answer. The reaction that my mind expects is so different from the reality of my heart. I have also got to the point where I can now feel what my heart is saying without having to stop and quieten myself. It is like I am now guided by its wisdom rather than my mind. Getting to this point has allowed me to know that at each decision point I am making a choice that is right and from my heart instead of from my intellect.

My heart knows how I really feel about a situation, and my gut tells me what I should do about it.

Your heart is the greatest resource you have, so before you reach for Google, check in with your heart and you will be amazed at the depth of knowledge, understanding and compassion that lies there. I am regularly blown away by what my heart has to tell me regarding how I should act. I can sit in meditation with my heart and feel peace, or joy, or I can have tears rolling down my cheeks as I experience an old hurt that I have stored away for years that I am now ready to face and release. Each experience is different, but each time I step away from my meditation with more compassion, more ability to let go, and more humility for the gift of life that we have been given.

• • •

The next step was to connect my heart to others. Sinking into the well of my heart, feeling the mix of emotions, the joy, the fear, the ambition is tremendous, but it is tough to then decide to show this to others. Being vulnerable is not widely accepted, but it is widely craved by everyone. That vulnerability allows us to connect heart to heart, it allows us to build bonds of love, compassion and trust. This is one of the bravest steps I have ever taken.

• • •

Lesson: Listen to your heart; it can teach you more about what to do next than your head.

- Make it a habit each day to spend time focusing on your breath;
- Step back and take time to review a situation, understand how you feel, as well as considering the facts;
- Write down if there is any conflict between how you feel about a situation and how your head or experience is telling you to act.

HI, MY NAME IS HELEN AND I'M ADDICTED TO STRESS

I am a stress addict. It took me a long time to realise this, and now that I have, it is a habit I want to quit - fast - but I also know it will take time to recover. I am also starting to recognise the signs of stress addiction in a number of people around me, as well. I had been struggling with writing and had not put any words on paper for nearly a week, when I decided to give myself a break and just use my usual writing time to journal. Below is the output of those days. Initially, I thought it would have no value to this book at all until I had my lightbulb moment that my addiction to stress was the most significant barrier to me successfully living from love. Therefore, I have kept these few days of journaling as part of the book, as I hope they will act as an insight into my addiction, and maybe help you identify if you share them.

Like any addiction, stress let me hide away from the world. It gave me excuses I could validate to myself and seemed justifiable to others around me.

24th March
There is something about the modern corporate culture that is toxic. It may not just be in the corporate world, but that is where I experience it most starkly. We pressure people into such a state of stress to deliver results that we wrap in fluffy words to make us feel better about ourselves, but that, in essence, just makes rich people richer for the sake of making them richer. There are a few of the elite who do great things with their wealth, but I question if the majority will leave this planet with any lasting legacy that befits the numbers of lives they have crushed and potentially ruined.

I know I may seem extremist, but how many people do you know who are stifling their creativity because they won't take a risk on their dream because they have to pay the mortgage? How many relationships have suffered due to excessively long hours and days away from home for a job that does nothing?

I am in an industry that proclaims it changes lives, but we do it for a very healthy profit and at the expense of the happiness and well-being of our staff.

I am currently writing this in a hotel room whilst my partner and youngest son are in A&E. I am, again, away from home, on a priority visit to a partner to run an all-day workshop, instead of being there with my youngest, holding his hand and bringing him comfort.

Too often we ask our staff to sacrifice what should be critical to them for the bottom line. Here I am, writing a book about love and leadership, feeling as though I have let everyone down and not being strong or brave enough to throw in the towel and say, "enough is enough."

But someone has to at some point. Who will be the catalyst to the change we so desperately need to see? I would love to be part of that movement, and for the right moment of inspiration and timing to present itself. But how does that change happen? What is the tipping point for the social enterprise? I am not sure if I am a believer in a standard living wage or complete parity of earnings, but I do know that what we have now is unsustainable.

Egos driven by fear beat down on other egos further down the hierarchy and so it keeps on perpetuating itself across an organisation. As a team leader, I try to set an example of the buck stops with me. I am the person who will take the blame, fix the problem and support the team to be home to their families in time for tea, but the one person I can't seem to do it for is myself.

Standing up for myself and what I personally believe in seems to be something that I find incredibly difficult to do. I know I still have a lot of work to do on myself in this regard, and I need to learn to set boundaries with those around, especially at work, if I am going to give myself the space to be the best I can be. How can I start saying "no" without sounding weak or unable to cope with the pressures of an executive job?

I have given myself a task to give myself a break and say "no" more. My plan is to track my next 30 days, as I learn to set up space and time in my life for the things that are truly important: my boys, my partner and my friends; whilst at the same time, doing a job that is delivering what my business needs me to deliver.

25th March

It is an odd concept saying "no". I am not sure if we humans are programmed to please others so that we stay part of the tribe and get the protection and sustenance that that provides, but there are very few people I know who can say no effectively.

Early on in my career, I was advised to say yes to every opportunity, as you never know where it might lead, and you were more or less guaranteed to learn something. As I have advanced, I now see that as poor advice. We need to evaluate every opportunity against where we are trying to get to in life. We need to ensure that if we say yes, we are saying yes for the right reasons, and because it supports our growth and our personal learning. Not because it will please others and, therefore, make us look good. Saying yes to everything also risks turning us into busy fools, instead of making deliberate choices that support what we are trying to achieve with our lives.

But it is a tricky balance. I learnt a lot from those experiences when I was younger and I am also not sure I would have known how to accurately evaluate an opportunity that was going to teach me from one that was going to distract me from what I am trying to achieve in my life.

Even to this day my priorities are all too readily put on the back burner for the demands of an employer, as the priority to earn outweighs the priority to spend time with my children. People often tell me that I am creating an amazing life for my kids and I am setting an example of a strong working mother. But the flipside to that, is that on a daily basis I am sacrificing my time with them to earn something that, in itself, has no intrinsic value apart from what we put on it as a society.

And at what point am I just kowtowing to society's expectation of the super-woman, to prove that I am unbreakable and that I can have it all? So, how do I evaluate every opportunity?

I read a book a number of years ago called Dice Man, about a man who let the roll of dice determine his fate completely. The roll decided what he ate, where he lived and what he did on a daily basis. Now I am certainly not advocating that as a methodology, but how we do classify an opportunity. How does the heart decide over the head? This book is about living from your heart, so how does a heart evaluate?

Are we purely lead by our emotions? The psychology behind buying and selling certainly suggests we are, so why not let my heart decide when I say no and when I say yes? So, tomorrow I am going to spend an hour with my to-do list and I am going to let my heart choose if I say yes or no. I am going to let it lead me. It is going to be interesting to see when I get fearful over one of my heart decisions. At what point will my head start pushing back and tell me that I must conform?

Letting my heart decide doesn't mean I stop doing things, but it means I do the things that feel right.

30th March

There are times when I am not sure that life is worth all of this hard work. Surely it would be easier just to coast and let life lead you to where it takes you. I do think there is something in that for me. I have always pushed myself hard. I see myself as a high performer, an overachiever, and with that has come some great advantages, but there is also a lot of stress and a lot of hard work. As I am learning how to say "no" and to give myself a bit more space to think, feel and be, I wonder if I just need to give in and embrace the flow.

But I am not too sure what that looks like on a day to day basis. Like the Dice Man, do I wake up and just go with the roll, or see what appears in my inbox, or what feels like the right thing to do. Or does relaxing and going more with the flow of the universe mean prioritising my tasks more effectively and just doing the one at the top of the list, releasing any pressure I may put on myself to get them all done at once.

I think I spend a lot of time resisting this flow of the universe. To me, it feels lazy and wrong just to release and give in without a lot of striving to achieve, but I know with this resistance comes stress, and I definitely move through cycles of stress. I start letting go. I start relaxing and doing what is most vital, and then the moment I feel that I am back in control, I pile on the pressure and the tasks on the to-do list until I am at a point where I get so stressed for a week or so that I snap at people regularly and feel so overwhelmed that I spend the day close to tears.

This cannot be healthy. Why can't I learn to live more in a state of release and allowing? What beliefs and hang-ups do I have that force me to carry on pushing and pushing to the point of exhaustion?

I have been thinking and feeling a lot about these questions, and I know that if I'm completely honest with myself, these patterns are stopping me from becoming everything I want to be. They are stopping my flow of creativity, and they are hampering my ability to live from love.

I use tapping to release old habits or beliefs that no longer serve me, but I am finding it hard to articulate exactly what I need to release. I am addicted to stress and the attention it allows my ego to feel and get. Do I actually love the drama? I have never considered myself a drama queen, but maybe I secretly am? Maybe I have not let go of as much of my ego as I thought I had, I am still obviously firmly in its grasp, and it is ruling my life and potentially ruining it. I can now see that my love for stress and drama is stopping me from fulfilling my dreams. That is not something that I am willing to give up.

It is time for me to address my addiction to stress and the drama that comes with it.

Stress is a killer, we are beginning to see the scientific evidence of what emotional and mental stress does to our physical bodies, and it is terrifying. But it is also addictive. Stress is such a natural state for most people in the world that it garners a lot of sympathy and support. It's an excuse to drink too much and party hard. It is an excuse to bitch to our friends about our lives instead of being responsible for our emotional state. It blinds us to what we are and what we could become.

This week has taught me a tough lesson; I need to get a handle on my stress and stop letting it run my life. There is an old saying regarding meditation that if you don't have time for 10 minutes' worth of meditation, then you should do an hour. I had always thought that it was a rather pompous statement from smug monks, but looking back at this week, I now get it. It is telling us that if we genuinely think that we do not have even 10 minutes of a day for ourselves, then we are at a stress level that is unhealthy. I am starting to think that any level of stress is unhealthy – but, one step at a time.

Monday night was tough. I did not sleep well. I was stressed about work, about my little one and the fact that I was away. I tossed and turned in a hotel bed and Tuesday was even worse. I could not get my head straight, I snapped at my boss, and I wanted to strangle a colleague. I now see that all I needed to do was to have stopped, tapped and meditated on Monday, and I would have felt very, very differently the next day.

The most striking thing about stress is how it seeps into every aspect of our lives. It impacts our eating, our sleep, our productivity and our relationships, and whilst I logically knew these facts, my addiction is so strong, that I was seemingly happy to sacrifice these vital parts of my life to get an adrenaline high.

• • •

Exploring my stress addiction has been a fascinating journey so far, whilst I still have a long way to go before I reach the bottom of the issue and can truly say that I have gained control on my addiction, I have learnt a lot already. I am addicted not only to the stress of a big, high powered job, but also to the drama that can surround that. I am addicted to how people treat me differently, and especially, when I am stressed. People treat me with kid gloves and bend over backwards to make my life easier, and it only seems to happen when I am seemingly at the point of breaking.

I know that stress is an illusion. It is entirely of our own making. Unless I am being hunted down by a mountain lion, it is unlikely that my physical stress response is wholly warranted, and yet, I have grown accustomed to living in that state so that people will treat me in a way I want. Then when I get frustrated with being treated like a small child (which to be honest is how I am acting), I then pull myself together, reprioritise and relax.

It is an insane cycle to have got myself into, but I have mastered it over the last few decades. To a degree it helps my ego feel better about itself. It gives me something to complain about that others can relate to. I can whine about the pain in my shoulders, a by-product of too much stress, and people nod sympathetically and suggest I treat myself to a massage. What I actually need to treat myself to is a good talking to - in the right way, of course.

As I investigate each layer of my stress addiction, I am starting to see that there are barriers that I have built up, that also allow me to connect with people without actually having to be vulnerable and let them in. Stress enables you to engage with someone on common ground without having to share emotionally. We can be stressed, highly strung individuals and people know not to prod - they know to leave you alone; they instinctively know that they should not add any more stress. That has been a huge safety net for me over the years.

I am also wondering how quickly I can drop this addiction. How do you go cold turkey from stress? What could the side effects be? I certainly don't want to be curled up in a corner shaking, but I do want to let go of this false adrenaline which is running my life. If I drop stress overnight, will I lose motivation? Will I stop being a person who strives for my goals? Will I lose my ambition? I am intrigued by the answers to these questions. I know I want to move forward from this addiction, but unlike others, I am not sure what the benefits will indeed be. I don't know how it will change me as a person.

16th April

It has been nearly three weeks since I became aware of my addiction. It has been an interesting journey of self-awareness and tapping. There has been a lot of tapping! One of the fascinating aspects of my addiction has been the many ways I have used it to manipulate people around me. I had never noticed how much I used the drama of stress to get people to do what I wanted.

The disgust I felt at this realisation has led me to be acutely aware of my stress levels and how I am acting. That awareness has allowed me to step back and readjust my behaviour in a way that I have never been able to before. I have never really been one to fly off the handle, but when I have been stressed I just shut people down. Any offer of help is slammed, any kind gesture is battered away, and the poor person is made to feel like they have added even more of a burden.

I have found that in the last three weeks I have been more measured, calmer and much more able to go with the flow; and I have felt happier. I have enjoyed the little things more, I have taken advantage of the quiet moments to be quiet, and I have felt my shoulders relax in a way that I am not sure they ever have before.

I know my addiction is still there, I can feel it rear its head every so often, but I now know it for what it is. That means it has lost a considerable amount of power over me. I am not kidding myself that I will be addiction free overnight, but I have set the aim to reduce its hold on me each day.

The one side effect that I did not expect is that I am treating myself better. I am eating more healthily, walking more and generally being kinder to myself. I put that down to the heightened awareness, and I hope it lasts, as it feels good.

I also think my kids have noticed. I have felt closer to them over the last two weekends. I have felt more present, more with them and my bond with them seems to have grown stronger.

This next week will be the test though, as I am now away from home for the next 12 nights. How will my stress levels deal with the travel and solid work hours? I am hoping better than usual, but I am also not putting the pressure on myself to be perfect. I am allowed to still have bad days; I am human after all.

Lesson: Stress is addictive.

Stress is a socially acceptable and common addiction that many of us don't know we have. However, it can have a significant impact on how we act, perform and our relationships, that will not help us reach our potential.

- Are you addicted to the adrenaline and treatment that you receive when stressed?

- Journal your day for the next four weeks to see if any traits appear over time that you may not be immediately aware of;

- Find a method to allow you to manage your stress: tapping, exercise and meditation are all good suggestions – or, try all three;

- Be open with others about your stress levels, especially your family and your peers. They may have an insight into helping you manage your stress better that you cannot see.

STOP PLEASING PEOPLE

Pleasing people was a key driver of mine for many, many years. I thought the happier I made people, the more they would like me. But the reality was, that I don't think they noticed and all it did was make me unhappy, chasing other people's dreams, and not my own.

Pleasing people is often the easy option, it allows you not to have to form your own opinion, it seems the path of least resistance and it keeps you firmly within your comfort zone. An example we see so many times is how people vote. The number of people I knew growing up, and sadly still today, who vote the same way their parents do because that's what they have always done, is scary. It is easier just to follow than to sit down, read the policies and party manifestos, and form your own opinions based on your beliefs, not someone else's.

I also used to please people so they would approve of me and give me praise. I needed the validation that I was worthy and had value, and I gained this by doing things for others that I thought would please them. Every time I did, I diminished my worth and my value.

I now know that it was fear that was making me please people, fear that I didn't know who I was or who I wanted to be, so I was lost. Fear of not being liked for being me, fear of not being loveable, driven by abandonment issues from my father leaving when I was so young. Fear of not fitting in, fear of failing and becoming a laughingstock. It was so much easier just to play small, stay safe and do what people wanted me to do, or what I thought they wanted.

Pleasing people is exhausting; there is no rest, no end to the seeming demands, no space to breathe and step back. The number of times I have been close to complete emotional, mental and physical exhaustion because I have been trying to make everyone around me happy are countless.

This next comment may seem like a bit of a sweeping statement, but being a people pleaser seems to be more of a female trait than a male one, certainly in my experience, and definitely from what I have seen in the workplace. This thought intrigued me as I am not usually a believer in gender stereotypes, but there seemed to be a link, and I started wondering if this was about nurturing or compassion.

It was then that I started to understand that everything has an opposite - I know that sounds obvious but bear with me. If being brave enough to live your life on your terms rather than pleasing others can give you the strength to be genuinely compassionate, then if you are lacking that courage, you will naturally fall into pleasing people, as it feels the safer thing to do.

I feel very privileged to have been born female. As a gender, we have a unique strength and power that can move mountains and bring huge joy, connection and harmony to this world. If we believe in ourselves. I'm not saying men don't, but I think women undervalue the impact they can have a lot of the time, so we try and please. History has made us subservient and whilst the need for equality is critical, I do believe that equality is very different from being the same. There are basic hygiene factors, such as equal pay for the same job which need to be in place, but we also need to create a culture that celebrates difference, diversity and the huge value that these can bring. That is gender agnostic.

I was brought up in a dichotomy. My mother was proof that whilst a glass ceiling may exist, it could be smashed through by hard work and perseverance. My grandmother, on the other hand, felt she had been dealt a raw deal by being a woman. She did not know her place in the world or feel that she had many options available to her. I grew up knowing that in the workplace I could be anything I wanted to be, but at home I felt had to be subservient and serve others, and I was never sure of my role. I tried to be everything to everybody, and not only failed, but exhausted myself at the same time.

For all of my life, I have been more comfortable in the presence of men. I find them easier to deal with, more logical and stable. I found women complicated and emotional. This is no wonder considering how terrified of my emotions I have spent most of my life. I found it hard to engage and trust women, and I found it nearly impossible to trust my feminine side. To me, all those mushy feelings felt weaker and more unpredictable.

I went to an all-boys prep school. From the age of three, I was in an environment of about 120 boys and 18 girls. To a degree, we were all treated the same. We played rugby, slept in the same dormitories until we were about nine, and had no real concessions made for gender. Skirts seemed to be the only noticeable acknowledgement of any difference.

I remember one bizarre concession that was made for the girls. It was decided by one of the elderly female teachers that girls needed more exercise than boys, and so, every day we had to do ten lengths of the swimming pool on top of every other activity we did.

There was one day when this clashed with the trials for Sports Day. I had made it to the semi-final of the 100-metre sprint, but because I also had to do my ten lengths, I ran the heat, soaking wet, in my swimming costume. Weird as that seems now, back then it seemed perfectly normal, but as I grew older, it has stuck out as my first real experience of gender discrimination. I came second in the heat and made it through to the final, but I also remember the stinging embarrassment of walking back up to the changing rooms in nothing but my swimming costume and all because someone had decided girls needed more exercise.

Shut down as I was, I was happy in my antiquated boarding school. It was neat, it was structured, and I could understand how I fitted in. I knew what my role was and how to play it. At the age of eleven, I was thrown into chaos. That may seem like an extreme exaggeration, but the terror I felt at finding myself in an all-girls school, my body changing and having no safety net or framework in which to ground myself, set me into a spiral of denial and self-hatred. I survived my first year, miserable, alone and not understanding why this was happening to me. But I was going to continue to be the good girl that I knew I should be. I would smile politely, tell everyone I was happy and go about my business hoping no one noticed how locked my heart was. And they didn't.

I was getting away with it, just. I remember being pinned to my bed by two girls as I was beaten by a third with a hairbrush, knowing that the calmer I was, the sooner it would go away. Night after night, I got better at being calmer as the abuse continued. I also felt that I deserved it, every cruel word they said was the truth, and every strike was warranted in some way. I thought so little of myself as a human being that I was entirely willing to put up with the bullying stoically. I started cutting myself with the blade from a pencil sharpener to try and feel something and I quickly became bulimic. But to the outside world, I was fine. I was passing my exams, and I was playing the part to perfection.

I blamed my stepfather for my pain. He was the one who decided an all-girls environment would be best for me, and that anger stewed, boiled and seeped into every cell of my body until I no longer felt anything. I now know the blame was unfair and I was equally complicit in my own situation. At any time I could have spoken up, but I was utterly convinced that no one would listen, that no one would care, that I would end up being a burden to those around me. So, I literally suffered in silence.

Luckily by 16, I had convinced my mother and stepfather that the teaching of science and maths was significantly better at the local state school, so I escaped the hell and the bullying from others, but not from myself.

After five years, the pattern of bullying and abuse was so ingrained that I carried on myself. Starving myself and then bingeing until I ended up throwing up everything in tears in our family bathroom.

I have never known what made me stop, but I was child-minding my cousins one summer when I was 17. I was bent over the sink in my bedroom bringing up the lunch I had just prepared for us all, when I caught myself in the mirror. I made eye contact with a person so hurt, so lost and so overwhelmed with self-hatred that I was shocked into the realisation of what I was doing to myself.

I never sought help, and I have hardly ever spoken about this time to even my closest friends, but that moment brought me to my senses enough for me to at least stop. That girl in the mirror still haunts me every so often. She reminds me of what I can do to myself when I shut myself down, when I lose myself by pleasing those around me, when I enter misery so completely.

As I look back on my life, it has been the lows - the points when part of me has caught myself about to hit rock bottom - that have clawed me back from the edge. I believe that part of me is love. The love I feel engulfs my heart now on a daily basis. The love that makes my eyes well with tears of gratitude and affection for the person I have become and the life I am privileged to lead.

But pleasing those around me, especially in the corporate space still feels like a daily activity for many women. It felt like an unspoken rule in the workplace that I had to work twice as hard and twice as long than any male colleague to be considered anywhere close to equal. The women I saw achieve and succeed, did so by sheer determination, grit and sacrifice. It did not, and still does not, feel like an even playing field. I was taught to succeed in the world of work like a man does, but I feel that we are missing the trick as women. We are not better than our male counterparts, but we are different, and we need to embrace that difference, learn to understand it, and use it to the advantage of those around us who we serve.

There is a strength in being a woman that is subtle, under-stated and yet, can bring the world to its knees in awe. There is a beauty and innocence to the way a woman can be both a nurturing force and a beacon of inspiration. It took me a long, long time to accept that I was a woman. I somehow felt it was inferior, less, weaker than being a man. I seemed to not forgive myself for having been born female; I railed against everything that was feminine; I resisted the enormous well of power that comes from the essence of femininity. The concept of giving into my vulnerability, and finding the immense strength and power that lies within it was inconceivable.

To stand in that power and let that flow into the world terrified me and my ego to its core. I nurtured and welcomed my masculine side until the point that it broke me. Amusingly, this happened after the birth of my second child. I was exhausted, sleeping only a few hours a night, trying to grapple with the fact that I was a mother, that people were dependent on me, that I had full responsibility for yet another life looking up at me with such love. I felt trapped, unable to cope with the love I felt or to pigeonhole it into a neat and rigid box. I felt that my entire being was crumbling around me, as if I had lost my identity, my life, my very being. The safety of my career and my work were not available, and I felt as though I had lost my anchor.

I did not know where to start, or where to turn. I could not voice what I felt or what was happening. There were no words, and there was no way anyone was going to understand or see me as anything but crazy.

That was the fateful day of the question about living from my heart. The day when I thought I could take no more, that this was close to the end of my wits, my strength, my tether. That day, I sat and cried my heart out into a cup of herbal tea. Living from your heart required me to understand what it is to be a woman. To understand the power of compassion, of the boundless love of the power of creation that we all hold. Embracing our feminine does not preclude the male gender, but I do think it is somehow tougher for men to acknowledge their vulnerability and surrender to themselves. I know a few men who have, and they are no less men, in fact, they are stronger, more able to support and more loving than many others.

Nor does it mean that all women have this ability innately. Like me, many have suppressed their power, out of fear, misunderstanding or ignorance, about the importance of the role we are put on this earth to play. The female power is here to heal; it is here to love; it is here to unite and connect us together. It is the reason that the mother is the core of the family, that we talk of Mother Earth and that most ancient cultures worshiped the female power of rebirth and creation. Creativity in itself comes from the very core of feminine power.

Learning to step into this power, this side of me, required me to let go of so much hurt and fear. To open myself up to being vulnerable to myself and to others and to be in a state of constant awareness of the power emanating from my heart.

My children awakened my power. They taught me the strength of love that I had never felt before, and I am not sure I will ever be able to show them the gratitude and appreciation I have for them.

• • •

The shift from masculine to feminine for me, was not the purchase of endless amount of pink clothing and décor, but a much more subtle exploration of compassion.

I had always been right, and if I wasn't, then I would go down fighting to ensure that, somehow, my ego retained its facade. I would feel personally wounded and wronged if there was the slightest chink in my armour, and the concept of learning by putting myself in another's shoes, was pretty alien to me.

Compassion is the root of feminine power, and it is the strongest and toughest skill to adopt. Being compassionate does not mean feeling what others feel, that is empathy, and whilst if we had more empathy in this world we would take a huge step in the right direction, it is not what we need to change our culture in the way it so badly needs.

Compassion is about understanding someone's perspective and doing everything within our power to do something to help them. Not to fix them, but to allow them to sit with their emotions, to create a loving space for them to truly express who they are. It is about understanding, about listening and about action. You cannot compassionately sit on the sidelines. If you truly have unconditional compassion, you have to throw yourself all in. As I started to explore compassion, I realised that I was happy with empathy and sympathy, I could even be compassionate to those I liked, but I really struggled when it came to people or situations that frustrated me or pushed my buttons.

Unconditional love and unconditional compassion are intricately intertwined. You cannot separate the two, and once you have embraced them, there is little you can do to stop yourself from acting, to do what you must to help someone through their suffering. Compassion is not about finding a solution or a fix, but the consistency of supporting another to find their path to joy and the freedom of being.

It is hard. It takes courage, vast amounts of dedication, and there are many days when I know I can do better. But for me, becoming compassionate is not about perfection; it is about striving each day to be better and better at pouring much-needed compassion into this world. Nor is compassion about doing and giving people what they want, or what they think they want. Compassion is about doing what is best for that person, that soul, and that can often be very different from what their ego wants.

Having made the decision to start bringing more compassion into my relationships, I knew I had to begin where it was both easiest and hardest; at home, before I looked to become a compassionate leader in the workplace.

Unconditional compassion at home should be natural, you are surrounded by those you love, you have an easy starting point, but you are also surrounded by those who know you the best and can press every trigger with skilled precision. What I realised was that I needed to give myself space to express emotions that my family brought up, in a way that still allowed me to be compassionate in my interactions with them. It meant a level of honesty about my needs that was refreshing and new. I had to learn to ask for my time to meditate or tap. I had to give myself the space to process whatever came up when it came up so that I could maintain compassion for those around me without it turning into an act.

It meant for the first time in my life not pleasing other people. I had to stand up and fight for myself, and that was scary as hell, as it meant I had to value my worth and myself.

As I started to understand that I needed to love myself, I quickly realised that there were definitely parts of me, and triggers I have, that I don't like. Even to this day, there are times when my mother calls and I can just feel myself shut down and not want to engage. Not all the time, but she knows when I am feeling stressed or unsure, and she has gained a serious level of mastery at pushing all my buttons at once, and I know she does it out of love and concern, but the triggers are still there.

I am never proud of myself when I get off the phone, but I know I need to work more on giving myself, and her, a break. To love myself, I needed to address the mask that I was wearing each and every day. I needed to look at my ego.

There are so many, good and bad, books written about the ego; what it is; how to control it or let it go; but for me, my ego is that part of my personality that wants to protect my self-image and how others perceive me. It is the part of me that shouts "look at me, aren't I great!" and it is usually shouting the loudest when I am the most afraid. It is my mask, my game face that I can hide behind and use as an excuse when situations get tough or scary. My ego is the part of me that runs from intimacy and honesty.

When I started meditating and getting a grip on my spirituality, I made a decision that I was going to "kill" my ego - a noble, but completely laughable, goal. I went on Buddhist retreats, I spent days in silence, meditating at 5 am to the sunrise and mindfully working my way through the rest of the day. But the reality is, that is not me. I am not quiet, and I am not an early riser, by nature. So, why was I trying to force myself to be? I tried guided meditation after guided meditation. I read every book I could find in a concerted effort to eradicate my ego. This was a battle I was going to win because my ego was BAD!

What utter BS!

It took me years to realise that the exact thing I was trying to eradicate was the part of me I was actually empowering by all this struggle. I was so hell-bent on being a dutiful, mindful and spiritual warrior, that I missed the entire point of spirit - acceptance.

We aren't put on this earth to all become the Dalai Lama. We aren't all meant to mindfully shuffle around in robes emanating pure compassion and presence to the world. We are put here to be the best versions of us we can possibly be. That means accepting that we aren't all perfect, or supermodels or geniuses. We are unique, one of a kind and there will only ever be one of us. We need to learn to accept, embrace and love every cell of that being.

Over the years of learning this lesson, I have come to understand that there are parts of me that are awesome, there are parts of me that are OK, and there are other parts that I would rather just forget about and ignore. But they are all me, and I need to accept them all.

• • •

In my opinion, there is no place where ego is more prevalent than in the workplace. The need for survival, advancement and recognition is built into our corporate culture. It is expected that individuals are out purely for their own gain. It is rare that you come across a leader at any level in the hierarchy who is truly doing what is best for their people, the business or the customer. We spend most of our work life trying to look better than others around us, and every aspect of corporate culture is there to reinforce that behaviour.

I was lucky enough to work for a leader who couldn't care less about comparing himself or his team to those around us. On the surface, most would say that his ego was alive and healthy, but once you got under the surface, what I saw was someone who was pretty impressive, with a heart and mind purely focused on his team and his customers. He stuck his neck out for his customers, he did what was right, and he fought his corner for his team. He got branded for it. "Oh, he's a maverick", "He can't be trusted", "He's not a company player".

How we push back on anyone who does not conform to our ideal of normal!

It may seem a little ironic considering that the majority of this book is about me and the life I have led, but one of the things I have noticed since living from love is that my story no longer matters so much to me. I was recently asked to tell someone about myself, and I was a little stumped. There are facts, I am a mum of two, I live in the UK, I am 42, etc. But my, apparently insufficient answer is that I am me. The joys and trials of my life have certainly helped me get to where I am at the moment, but they don't make me who I am. Who I am is a choice I have made. I have chosen to be someone who will love over hate, someone who will comfort rather than confront, and someone who wants to be happy and responsible for my life rather than a victim of circumstance or others' opinions.

This choice has not always been easy. There are times when I am tired that I want to be grumpy and snap. I still get stressed, and yes, my mum can still press all those buttons. But I have chosen that that is not who I want to be. I want to be someone who brings joy and a smiles to others. I no longer need, or seek, external validation from others because I get their sympathy or pity for what I perceive "I went through".

Letting go of my story has allowed me to let go of so much else. Caring about what people thought of me dominated my life. I spent nearly every waking hour thinking and giving my energy to caring what people thought, to questions I was never brave enough actually to ask. I was so preoccupied with the views of others, that I had no focus on what I actually wanted and what was truly important. I even spent significant amounts of time worrying about what people who had never heard of me would think of me.

I am still saddened sometimes, when I look back to some of the events in my life, when I was not there, I was not present, I had made choices to please others. My wedding was an example of this. I got married and had my wedding in the way I did to not upset people and to do what was expected. This saddens me as it was disrespectful to the wonderful and kind man who wanted to be my husband, and to all the guests who had put their time, energy and money into attending. It is also such as waste. Time is so precious, and it is the only thing that we cannot get more of, and yet, I was so willing to squander it by being mindless.

• • •

There is a scene in the movie Eat, Pray, Love, where the main character is walking through her house, and Julia Roberts is narrating. The gist of what is being said is that she was there for every decision that was made, every choice of countertop, every paint colour, every event, but she was never present. I remember watching that scene and dissolving into uncontrollable tears. Someone had just verbalised exactly how I felt. The fact that I was in economy class on a flight to Dubai was a little inconvenient, but it was the first time I remember really feeling that I didn't care what the other passengers thought. I was not going to pull myself together and get over it. I was going to feel and address the issue at hand.

The issue being, that I was deeply unhappy and had no idea what to do about it. The fact that I had dedicated my life to making others happy and making sure they had a good opinion of me, was not helping me. I had not made a choice that was purely for me.

I had built my life to the expectations that I assumed others had of me, and that is easy. It allows you to coast and play it safe. It gives you the opt-out clause of designing the life of your dreams. I let myself handover the reins of my destiny to the elusive "they". I could name them if pushed: my mother, my grandfather, my grandmother, my father, my teachers, my bullies - but it was bullshit. They had never sat me down and told me what they wanted me to do or be in my life. As an adult, it was time for me to take responsibility for me, and start figuring out what sort of life I actually wanted to live and lead.

Choosing to rise above basing your worth on the opinion of others, does not mean you become indifferent. In fact, I have found it has made me feel more. More joy, more loss, more happiness, more pain. I am in touch with how I feel, in that moment, and that can be intensely powerful and raw, but it is always real. The difference is, that I have decided that my emotions are exactly that; mine. They are not there for others to manipulate me with. I am allowed to feel how I feel and vocalise that to others in a way that is not designed to shape their opinion of me. Because the juxtaposition is true. If I no longer feel obligated to base my worth on other's opinion, I should not expect my opinion to dictate another's worth.

What I mean by this, is that I can no longer push my emotions and thoughts on another and expect them to change because of what I think. Sometimes, that is tough. Tough when you feel someone is being a jerk or not treating you how you would treat them and you cannot change that. You can state how hurt, annoyed, etc., you are but you cannot expect them to change. *You cannot manipulate people with your emotions.*

I remember when I was growing up, I was always being told I would disappoint someone if I didn't do something the way they wanted it to be done. This piece of emotional blackmail was used by nearly every adult in my life, and it was deemed to be OK. It is not. It is using your will to move someone in a weaker position to you. It is bullying. I know to most that may seem extreme, what harm is there if a teacher tells a pupil they will be disappointed if they don't revise hard and do well on an exam? Quite a bit actually. Instead of discovering a love for learning and expanding their curiosity, this pupil quickly equates the act of learning with that of gaining approval from others.

Good God is this prevalent in management nowadays. And yes, I have been guilty of it on more than one occasion. "Do this, or the company will suffer", "We can't let our customer's down!" Both pretty benign statements but what they actually say is "if anything bad happens it is your fault - not mine."

We can all get our message across in a way that uplifts people. "What can we do together to make this company thrive?" "What could we do to make our customer's love us more?" "How can I help you love this subject so much that you ace this exam?"

The outcomes we are trying to achieve are the same, but the path is so different. This new path requires awareness and planning. It needs you to be conscious of what you are saying and how it may be received and perceived by another. It needs you to love yourself enough that you are willing to go up against the norm.

Making this extra effort is hard. Being aware and present enough to really think before you speak requires discipline and a lot of planning. It also means letting go of that requirement to be perfect. I have found that I plan my messages a lot more. I think through what I say from every angle, making sure I am there to elevate the discussion and thought, not get everyone to agree with me. That is somewhat complicated in the modern world, where everything has to be done at warp-speed, or in 140 characters.

• • •

We currently live in a world where we are more connected and more disconnected than ever before. We are bombarded with information that we have to question, so we have started questioning everything we hear or read. Who can we trust is becoming a question that has increased in importance in my lifetime.

Growing up in the UK, we would never have dreamed of questioning the BBC news, yet today, everything I read on that site (as well as most others), I take with a pinch of salt. Everyone has a spin because everyone has their story that they are selling to twist you to their way of thinking. Think about it. Every post you write on social media is about projecting to the world how you want it to react to you. Your profile on LinkedIn, your groups on Facebook, are all there to allow you to get the approval and validation you require. Don't get me wrong, I think there are some huge benefits that social media can give us, but until we let go of our stories, we are all just online, seeking validation, instead of providing value.

The next time you post something, I want you to ask yourself, "Am I posting this to give value to others or get approval?" Don't post for "likes", post to touch hearts.

• • •

We all have our opinions, and that is something to celebrate and learn from, not a challenge to change others. People can change their mind based on new evidence and perspectives, but it should never be our aim to change someone's opinion. Our goal should be learning from another's view. Each of us is unique, and we each have our own story that made us who we are today. The joy in life is allowing yourself to be curious and learn from everyone's journeys, but not to be so attached to your own that it defines who you are in this world. So, please go out and find what really brings you joy.

What makes your heart sing? Who makes you laugh? Where do you feel safe? Where do you feel exhilarated? Get out your notebook, or open your laptop, now, and start building a list of the things you love and stick it on the fridge. Do you do something on this list every day? It doesn't have to be extreme; it can be as simple as spending an extra five seconds hugging your kids, kissing your partner, or stopping on the way to work to admire the beautiful architecture around you. Whatever it is, make a commitment to yourself now to start doing at least one thing every day that brings you joy, that pleases you, and watch as your life of wonder and joy unfolds around you.

I still catch myself every so often, thinking about how my actions may gain me approval from another. It is getting rarer, which is a good sign, but there are still times when something will come up and a learned response kicks in automatically. I now welcome these as they are great learning moments. I have chosen to not engage with these but to investigate them. Why did this response come up? What was happening? What was I thinking about? By digging into these instances, I have found a great way of uncovering the issues that are still unconsciously bothering me, and most of them are based within my old willingness to please those around me.

• • •

Lesson: Pleasing people won't help you succeed, but it will exhaust you and make you stressed.

Being liked is an excellent anthropological way of staying safe, but it limits our ability to become great leaders, as we are more likely to focus on the opinions of others, rather than innovate or form our own.

- If you are uncomfortable with saying "no", start with saying "yes, but…";

- This technique will allow you to set limitations or boundaries to what you will agree to. For example, "Yes, I can do that piece of work for you, but I won't be able to start it until next week as I have other priorities right now." Over time it will become easier to say "no".

- Spend time writing down what is important to you as this will give you a guide to help you determine whether you should say yes or not;

- If your superiors are pushing you to say "yes", request a specific meeting to sit down, discuss, document their priorities, and the current activities that you are working on. This process will highlight if there are any mismatches and allow you to focus your energy appropriately.

LOVE THE MOMENT

There are moments that define us. We can either embrace the lesson, accept the fact we may need to face our fears and make a change, or, we stay on the path or in the rut that we have created for ourselves. I have had a number of defining moments in my life and I have not always been brave enough to engage with the message they are trying to deliver. These are the points when I now reflect and understand that the pivotal decision I made was in that instant. Hours of thought, deliberation and conversation may have been needed to get me to that point, but it is the moment the decision is made, along with my commitment, that the magic happens.

Sat on a beach in Sri Lanka, staring out over the ocean, feeling like I was on the edge of the world, was one of those split-second moments. The moment I decided only the big things matter, the moment I decided that even after a year of serious change and growth that I wanted more. I wanted to face my demons; I wanted to create a life of vast and defining aspirations. The small facts don't matter only the bigger picture of what could be, of what I could be.

It is all about letting go, surrendering and trusting the moment; the instant.

At that moment, looking out at the ocean, with nothing between me and Antarctica, I was finally willing to make that choice. I honestly don't know how any of this will roll out. I don't know what my next step will be, but I am going to trust that the universe does. My commitment is that I will stay as present and as grounded in love as I can be and that the kids have to come an equal first to my dreams and happiness.

Being present, mindful, and living in the moment - There are so many religious teachings, books, apps, courses, and even movies, that talk about the power of the Now. There is even the book "The Power of Now" by Eckhart Tolle. Most of us have heard of it at some point in our lives. But it is bloody difficult. Making the decision that you are going to become more mindful is one thing, but it does not turn off the constant nattering in your head or your ego. There is a reason why monks and nuns dedicate their lives to the mastery of mindfulness because it takes that level of commitment.

The first step towards being mindful is to give yourself a break! You will not get good at this - the only goal you should be aiming for is progress. Anything more than that and you are setting yourself up for failure.

• • •

When I decided I was going to lead a more mindful life, I packed myself off to a Buddhist retreat in the South of France, and ended up pissed off and frustrated that I could not grasp this seemingly simple concept immediately. The first morning, I bounced out of bed for 5 am meditation, only to spend 60 minutes squirming on a meditation cushion attempting not to scream, as the pins and needles in my legs felt like red hot daggers being plunged into my calves. Needless to say, the rest of the week continued to go as well as the first session, until day four when a few of us decided we had had enough of silent vegan meals and hard work in the rain. So we made a break for it to the local French bar and partook in a lot of red wine and pizza!

Over the afternoon, we started to share our experiences of the week and our fears about the fact that we just could not do it right. We shared how we were berating ourselves for the lack of ability to implement such a simple practice, as we slowly got drunker and drunker, and more and more open. Bizarrely, that was the breakthrough moment for me. We got back to the monastery, passed out in our beds and hauled ourselves to mediation the next morning.

Sitting on that cushion, struggling with the kind of hangover that only bad, cheap French red wine gives you, I decided that I was just going to survive. I was going to go from breath to breath, attempt not to vomit or pass out, and, eventually, the gong would chime. And it did, in what seemed like five seconds. I was so intensely focused on breathing, so intent in getting that simple action right, that the time flew by.

I am not claiming that the path to enlightenment starts in a French bar, but for me, it was definitely a step in the right direction.

The rest of the retreat was a joy, I had dropped all expectations, and I was just enjoying the time to relax and engage with the people around me. I discovered that nuns really don't take themselves very seriously and that clearing a lotus pond in the pouring rain could actually be a lot of fun. My point is, when you start to bring mindfulness into your life, do it gently, without expectation and with a lightness of heart.

The moment is such an astonishing second of beauty and wonder. In the moment everything is clear, pure and innocent. It is only when we step into the future or fall back into the past that we add our judgement and assign label such as good, bad or indifferent. Us humans are amazing creatures, without our memories or our imaginations we could never have survived to evolve and advance as we have. Yet, this can come at a cost. And that cost is the fear, regret or anxiety that most people live their entire lives in.

In today's modern world, the majority of us are physically safe, so our semi-permanent state of fight or flight is down to our planning for the future or burdens we have given ourselves from our past. We put ourselves into such a state of on-going stress, by choice, that stress is rapidly becoming a significant health concern. It is only by learning and committing to the habit of the moment, that we can bring lasting joy and peace back into our lives. This is a point I want to stress (excuse the pun) - the state of stress we live in is something we do to ourselves. We have chosen to be stressed - you - not anyone else. So you can change it. Yes, life can be tough sometimes, but your presence will transform or destroy how you experience any situation. Stress is of our own making, and we can now choose to walk away from it, once and for all.

I start my day, or at least I try (it is not always possible with two small boys), by being present as I wake. I feel the comfort of the mattress beneath me supporting my body, the warmth of the duvet and the softness of the pillow. I lie there with my eyes shut, feeling the breath enter and leave my body, whilst trying to notice every sensation in my body. Feeling the growing urge to stretch and then I notice how the duvet slides over me as I do. Next, I lie and listen, what can I hear? Most mornings, it is at this point when I hear the muttering and giggling from next door, and I know it is time to get up and start breakfast. But the key is that I have started the day awake and awakened.

This simple routine has become a habit, no matter where I am in the world, I notice how I wake up, and it always sets me up for the day. The rare occasions I race out of bed without a moment of presence, I know I will struggle to ground myself for the rest of the day, unless I can find a space to meditate. Just spending two to three minutes each morning getting into the right frame of mind allows me to approach my day with love and peace. My attitude is my choice. Many people claim they are victims of circumstance, and whilst some people have the misfortune to be in a harsh environment, your frame of mind dictates how you experience it.

It is your choice to stay, or it is your choice to change.

I believe that choice and presence are intrinsically linked. When we live in the past or the future, we are giving away our ability to choose. We are replaying events and emotions, usually with a critical reflection on ourselves, and we are losing our ability to choose how we experience and associate with a memory. Instead of a memory being the pureness of what happened, we add commentary, additional hurt and slight or piles of "what if's". At that point, we have chosen to allow our interpretation of that memory to drive our current state of mind and mood. The same can be said of living in the future, either fearful of what might happen or overly optimistically dreaming, deprives us of the ability to choose how we are in the moment. Instead, we tend to move through life in a sort of fog that clouds our judgement and our choices, and we think that is perfectly normal.

How we are and who we are is our choice to make in any moment, we can be the engaged and present parent, or we can be distracted on our phones whilst the kids play alone. We can choose to actively listen to a friend and co-worker so that they feel heard and understood, or we can determine what we want to say next whilst others share their views and feelings. Our presence in the moment defines who we are and how people experience us.

Presence and choice both require discipline and practice. It is easy to drift through life disconnected and disengaged, allowing others to choose your path or your purpose. Or you can decide that each day you will live life in the moment, growing your presence from just a second or two, through to a minute and then five, ten, thirty, an hour. Making deliberate choices that serve you and the person you want to become. Meditation is a powerful tool to accomplish both. Regular meditation helps you learn to be more in each moment and starts to build the ability to ground yourself in the present. As you spend more time present during your daily life, you will begin to become more aware of the choices you make and those you give away to others to make for you. As you start to distinguish the two, you can mindfully decide how and when you want to take back your power to choose.

The amount you are present defines what you give to the world. If you are present, mindful of your choices and deliberate in what you do, you are giving the world and all those around you the best you can be. You are contributing from a place of love, joy and connection.

Many people are struggling with their purpose or their sense of belonging. They don't feel that they know why they are here or what they can give to the world. But this is because they do not allow themselves to learn to be present and to learn to face the fears that may arise from making choices in the moment.

What do I mean by that? Let me give you an example. For most of my childhood, I never felt that I had any friends. I certainly didn't have a "bestie" that I was inseparable from for any length of time. I never felt I could relax and be myself around others, so I was always guarded, nervous about not being perfect, terrified of letting others down, and therefore, failed to let anyone connect with me in any meaningful way. At some point in most people's lives, they have a moment like this. For others, like me, it is the majority of their life. They are so tightly wound with the pressure of pleasing those around them, that all of their choices are based on what will please another, rather than what would bring them joy or peace. I spent so much of my time in the pursuit of a best friend, that all I did was try and please those around me. I was not present with them, at any point, as all I was doing was living in my head, trying to figure out what would make them happy, instead of listening, or trying to figure out what would make me happy.

I am not talking about becoming selfish, but I am asking you to start putting yourself first. Understanding how you can love and support yourself allows you to become the best version of you. That will enable you to be more loving, more fun, more creative, more productive and better for everyone in your life. We have bought into a lie that we must serve others to the detriment of ourselves. Yes, we must serve. But we must first look to ensure that we are loving and kind to ourselves.

It is why when you have a new-born baby you are told to sleep when the baby sleeps. No mother really wants to, you feel like you must tidy the house, have a shower or do some work. But the reality is, if you cannot get the sleep you need, you will burn out, become exhausted, grumpy and not the mum that you want to be. I learnt this lesson the hard way and it was a great introduction to self-care.

I had decided at a very young age that the way to please people the most was to put everyone else before me. To be self-less, to meet others' expectations or needs, to try and please, please, please. For over thirty years, I did not ask for help or say what I wanted to say for fear of upsetting people. The person I was upsetting the most was myself. I was permanently exhausted and stressed, and I felt that I was completely undeserving of anything that remotely looked like support or care. It was not until after the birth of my first son that I learnt the lesson that I needed to look after myself and sometimes put me first. To this day, it is a discipline that I have to remind myself of regularly.

Self-care, for me, starts again with the mindful awareness of what state am I in. I live a wonderfully busy life, and it would be easy to bounce from one activity to the next without taking the time to check in with myself. But I have to come back to myself on a regular basis to see how I am. Am I tired? Stressed? In need of exercise, fun, relaxation? Allowing myself to stop, close my eyes, feels my toes on the floor and the breath coming in and out of my body, gives me a very good indication of what state I am in. I then give myself a score on a scale of one to 10. One, I am relaxed and present, 10, I am stressed and about to break. Once I have a number, I can then determine what I need to do. Anything over a four, and I sit down, do a tapping meditation and let myself relax. Anything under four and I know I am good to carry on going as my stress levels are not going to be a distraction. Anything over a seven and I look to booking a day off. I know it may seem extreme, but when I get to a seven and above, I know I need a day of rest, relaxation, meditation and time in nature. Nothing else will lower my stress enough.

It is rare that I get to a seven or above, but it is a very clear call to action from my body. If I ignore it, I know I will end up getting ill, which really gets in the way of living a life of love and joy! Putting yourself first and getting back into a state of health is an excellent expression of self-love as well. The stronger, more relaxed and more present you are, the more you can love and give to those around you.

Three Circle Exercise

We all have times in our lives when stress builds as quickly as the to-do list, and it is difficult to know what to do next to make a difference. I have come across many tools in my time, but the one that I use the most I like to call my three circles. I love this due to its simplicity and it allows me to see what I can actually do to change the situation.

On a large board, flip chart or three pieces of paper, draw three circles; label them Control, Influence and Surrender.

The Control circle is all the actions or situations that you have direct control over. i.e. you can do something to change the outcome. It is within your control, and therefore, you can choose to do it or not. The Influence circle is where you put all the items on your list that you need others to help you complete or action. The Surrender circle is for all the things that you would love to be able to solve but actually cannot.

For me an example for each circle would be:

- Control: My exercise regime or my attitude - I have complete control over this. It is my choice how and when I exercise, and I need to take responsibility solely for the choices I make. No one can exercise for me or choose how I turn up each day;

- Influence: My team's motivation level - I can set the culture of my team and create an environment which allows them to thrive, but I cannot choose for them how they show up each day and neither do I have control of their entire lives. I can help them make choices, but I cannot choose for them. The same is true for the happiness of my friends and family;

- Surrender: Brexit or the global economy - I can have an opinion and care about the outcome, but I have no direct control over the process itself. I can either expend energy grumbling about something I cannot control, or let go and trust that the process will work itself through and I will play my part when I need to.

Take your to-do list or a list of things that are bugging you and start writing each one in a circle that best fits. Once you have put everything in a circle, I then like to take the Let Go and Trust paper, and throw it away. I know it sounds foolish, but the act of screwing up a piece of paper or wiping the board clean is cathartic, and symbolically tells me that I am not longer wasting my time and energy on those things.

The next circle I tackle is Control. Look at the list you have created and ask yourself again, is all this honestly in my control only or are there items on this list that should belong in the Influence circle (there are usually one or two). Once I have done a quick sanity check, I take each item, and on a new piece of paper detail each action that needs to happen to complete each item. That is my focus for the day.

I then do something very similar for the Influence circle, however, as well as writing all the actions, I also write all the people I need to help me to complete them.

By compartmentalising my energy, I know that I can focus in a way that will be productive. It stops me from being the busy fool and allows me to deliver in a smart way. It also lowers my stress. Like many alpha types, I tend to be a control freak when stressed, so getting clear on what I can and cannot control allows me space to breathe.

Lesson: Your energy is finite; focus on the activities that make a difference and that you can control.

Life can be wasted if you spend too much time thinking about the past or the future. By staying as present as possible, you can make the best decisions to support you in whatever you are trying to achieve.

- Be honest with yourself about what you can do and what you cannot, no one is Superman or Wonder Woman, so we need to be conscious and deliberate about where we focus our energy;

- Create rituals to help you let go. By symbolically destroying a list of actions you can't complete, you are letting your subconscious and conscious mind know that they do not need to worry. It may seem peculiar at first, but there is incredible power in performing a physical ritual to let go mentally;

- Be open with your team and peers about what you can and cannot do. By promising to deliver everything, you are setting yourself and your team up for failure.

BUILD YOUR BOUNDARIES

Back in that field in Cambodia, I didn't know who I was or what I stood for, and it haunted me for years. The question of which side I would have been on, if I had been in a situation like the Khmer Rouge genocide in Cambodia, niggled at me, as I knew I was too busy pleasing those around me to be brave enough to stand up for what I thought was right. But it struck me as impossible to understand what I would stand up and fight for if I did not know my worth or what I stood for.

We talk a lot at work about values, and in fact, most of the companies I have worked for, have had a set of company values that are banded around like mascots, in a vague attempt to make people feel better about coming to work every day.

There is only one company where I can say those values were truly felt, and it is one of the largest and most successful companies in the world. I attribute a lot of that success to the fact that the staff, as one, knew who they were and what it stood for to turn up to work every day. It was the heartbeat of who we were and how we treated each other, as well as our customers and our partners. It gave us meaning, it gave us the courage to fight if needed and it gave us a code to live by. It was far more than vague marketing speak or good posters to have around the office.

It was there that I realised that I needed to build my own set of values, ones that would give me courage and meaning, and would support me to be the person that I wanted to be. All well and good, but alongside stopping pleasing people, this meant learning also to say "no". For me, learning to say no allowed me to also work out for the first time exactly what I wanted to say yes to.

That meant not only having values, but also knowing my limits. I can dive into things completely; I can get wrapped up in a challenge or opportunity that I can become obsessed to the point of doing very little, especially at work. The challenge of figuring out a solution to a problem and then implementing it can consume me. This is great in one way as I tend to get things done, but it means that I am not very good at balance, so I can lose myself, or become disconnected from other parts of my life. For short periods or for critical reasons, people can understand this, but do it for long enough and I found that the balance tips so far to one side that you risk losing so much: health, friendships and even marriage, in my case.

So setting my values and knowing what I stood for, also meant knowing what I was willing to be and do, as well as comprehend what I was not willing to do and be. It gave me a framework where I could test and validate opportunities and situations. It gave me a bar to measure against. It let me know what I would be willing to compromise in order to achieve a greater good.

These evolved over time, and I know they will continue to do so, but the set of values I have for myself are:

- I will do what I believe is the right course of action for those involved in the long run;

- I will not compromise myself to please another;

- I will continue to work on myself until I am able to authentically and honestly be the best version of me;

- I will treat others how I want to be treated, and I will be clear with others about what I expect.

Whenever I am now in a situation where I need to check in with my values, I sit, calm myself and start to meditate on these four statements. Sometimes it works better when I use them as questions, for example, am I trying to please someone rather than stand up for what I know is right? This questioning allows me to feel my way through the situation, to scenario plan what the potential outcomes could be. It also enables me to make conscious and deliberate choices.

Sticking to my values has not always been easy, and it has, on a regular occasion, forced me to make choices that others have questioned the validity of, but it has given me strength. It has also allowed me to respect the values of others - we don't all live by the same code, so we need to respect that. I have found that most people share similar values to me, and that has allowed us to work together successfully. But where there has been a difference that cannot be resolved, I have found it best to walk away.

I have also learnt to trust my gut more. There is a straightforward exercise that I use all the time. The more I do it, the faster I get at interpreting what my gut is trying to tell me.

I was once told that my body knows all the answers well before my head does. I still, to this day, don't know how, but I do now know it is true.

Sit down and close your eyes. Take five deep breaths, counting to four on the inhale and six on the exhale. Slowly bring your attention to your body. Where are you tense? Where do you feel relaxed? Carry on breathing deeply and letting the tension flow out of your body. When you are feeling relaxed and calm, bring your focus to your gut. Is your gut feeling relaxed or tense? If you feel tension there, carry on breathing and slowly let this tension release.

Once you feel relaxed ask yourself the question that has been worrying you. For example, "Can I trust this individual?" or "Is this the right house/job/car for me?" You can either say this in your head (preferable in public places) or out loud. Notice the reaction in your gut. Does your gut stay relaxed or is there a tightening? Any tightening is your body giving you a clear sign that it is not comfortable with the situation. Our gut reaction is there for a reason; learn to listen to it, and it becomes an incredible tool that can help you navigate complex situations and remain authentic to who you really are.

There have been times during tough negotiations or even interviews, that I have excused myself, gone somewhere quiet and tuned into my gut to get the answer I need, and it has never let me down.

Start small, choose an area of your life that you want to improve. Maybe it is cutting down on coffee or playing less Candy Crush (TM). Whatever it is, the moment you find yourself thinking "one more cup" or "just another level", still yourself with your breath, and ask yourself what you should be doing. The right answer will be there; we just have to be strong enough to listen and follow through.

Learn to love your gut and the innate knowledge it can provide. It will help you keep your boundaries and live up to your values.

• • •

Lesson: Knowing what you stand for will give you power to make the choices you need to make you succeed.

Once you are happy to say "no", you need to know what you want to say "yes" to, with all your heart.

- Write down the main activities you spend your time on each day. Are there any that are just distractions? Relaxing by reading a good book is great, but spending hours binge-watching TV or playing games on your phone are stopping you from achieving everything you want to;

- Get real with yourself and take responsibility for how you spend your time;

- Share your values with others, so that it is easier to explain to them the decisions you are making;

- Create team values and debate them. Make sure that they resonate with each member of the team and become a code you can all operate by.

INTEGRITY AND AUTHENTICITY

I have been lucky in my life and career, that I have worked for people who I both want to emulate and those who I want to be the polar opposite of. Being aware of the people around me, who influence me, has made me conscious about the behaviours and habits I have adopted. It has always bemused me how most people completely lack this conscious awareness of their behaviours and habits. It may be due to the fact that I have always judged myself so severely, that I also have an awareness of other's behaviours. Whatever the reason, it has proved to be a great learning tool.

One of the managing directors I worked for early in my career was, in his heart, a decent human, but was so ruled by his ego that any victory was all down to his genius and any defeat brought his wrath on the team. I remember watching him at his best, in full flow speaking at an event, enthralled by his passion and knowledge, and wishing that he had the self-awareness actually to see himself for what he truly was. He was brilliant, geeky and a lexicon in his field. But he wanted to be "The Boss" and anything that undermined this view of himself was unacceptable. To this day, I still wonder how successful he could have been if he had only stuck to his strengths and passions.

Conversely, what happened was that the business started to suffer, the staff began to leave in droves, and eventually, he went bust. He so stubbornly refused to give in to what he loved doing that he suffered in the long term. The first lesson I took from that experience was about the person I did not want to be, but over time and with maturity, I realised that the real lesson was around integrity and authenticity. He did not have integrity in his actions and no authenticity in his behaviours.

Integrity to me is a vital part of leading with love.

The classic definition of integrity, as we use daily, is around honesty, ethical principles and sticking to our morals, but I also love the dictionary.com secondary definition:

• • •

Integrity - the state of being whole, entire, or undiminished.

• • •

As a love leader, we must be whole, entire and undiminished. We must live and lead our lives in a way that is undiminished by our egos, entirely focused on our goals, our passions and for a cause we can wholly commit ourselves to.

Leading with integrity requires us to love without condition. It requires for the love we show to our jobs, our colleagues or our family, to be undiminished by the filters that we have adopted. It also requires us to be our whole selves at all times, not playing the part that may be expected of us. I demand that I stay as present as I can, but that doesn't mean that I am the best me all of the time. I can be tired, grumpy, or, even worse, hungry, and that will lower my performance levels, and that is OK. Integrity and authenticity don't expect perfection, they ask for honesty. I have to be honest with myself and others. It is OK to say "Sorry, I am really tired/upset/hungry today, so whilst I will try to give you my best answer/performance/time, it may not be as good as it would be after a great night's sleep."

Every time we interact with someone, we are making a choice, either to be coming from a place of love or a place of ego. By a place of ego, I mean from a mindset that is supporting our external image rather than what is best for all involved in the situation. Having integrity means not diminishing love, or the opinions and choices that others have made. Integrity means unconditionally allowing someone to be themselves. Each interaction we have, each conversation or conflict can be transformed by leading from love. By being open and honest about how we are feeling during each interaction removes the ego and the fear of judgement by others. It also gives you more support during the days when you are not at your best!

This is where my former boss went wrong. He allowed his passion and abilities to be diminished by the filters he chose. He decided a role for himself that did not allow him to be congruent with who he truly was. He chose to support the image he wanted to portray to the world, rather than choose to be his best self.

Authenticity was another part of the lesson I learnt. For me, there is something very visceral and emotional about authenticity. Our gut tells us a lot about people, if we listen to it, our "gut-dar" if you will. The inner knowing that something or someone is wrong, is powerful, and the key to our authenticity. If we want to be respected or followed, we need to be authentic, we need to ensure that the behaviours and messages we are delivering are in alignment with who we really are, otherwise, people's gut-dars will be on high alert. Being able to tune into your gut and understanding what it is trying to tell you, will help you understand if you are authentic to yourself.

Being authentic doesn't mean I am sharing my deepest thoughts in every conversation or interaction, but it means that I am openly who I am in that moment, not playing the role that may be expected. Many of us have been taught that we need to follow the textbook to lead effectively, but those rules don't allow for life, so we play the role of leader or manager to hide our weaknesses. Sadly, this often disconnects us and means we are not as effective as we could be as leaders. It is OK to let the mask fall completely and it is OK to still be learning - that is what makes life fun after all!

• • •

Lesson: Don't let fear stop you from being who you are. Accept that you are not perfect and never will be.

Compartmentalising ourselves to fit other people's expectations stops us from being brilliant.

- Your intuition is a powerful tool, use it. Data is great, but if it doesn't feel right, listen. As your intuition is always right!

- Step back from any situation that feels inauthentic, spend time writing down why you feel this way to determine what information you may be missing;

- Being yourself is a strength, not a weakness. It means you are learning and growing, and it makes you a great leader;

- Encourage your teams to be open about their concerns - let their guts have a voice as well.

TOUGH LOVE AND CONFLICT

Love is not weak, love is not a doormat, love does not compromise, but love is compassionate, listening and understanding. Love does not sit there with a smile on her face in submission. Love sprints headfirst into action.

OK, so I preach and live through love, but I am not a walk over. I don't float around in hippy dresses and smell of Patchouli oil. I am strong, fiercely independent and I am bloody successful at business. And sometimes, you end up in a situation where you need to be tough and ruthlessly focused on what is right.

So, how the hell do you lead with love when you are terminating someone's contract, making someone redundant, or putting someone on a performance improvement plan? To begin with, I struggled with these aspects of my life. I felt that I was a hypocrite or a traitor to the cause of love. I felt that, again, I had to put on a mask that allowed me to play a role to get the job done, rather than being the "me" I had grown to love.

During this struggle, I lent on my professional training, I justified, and I fell straight back into my old habits and behaviours. How can I love someone who is under-performing, misbehaving or plain incompetent? The reality is that parents do it all the time, but in the workplace, it is challenging to move from frustration into a place of love. No matter what most business leaders say about caring for their people, when the shit hits the fan, everyone becomes a line on a spreadsheet.

Leading with love and compassion is one of the hardest things that you will ever do. It requires faith in what you are doing and an absolute determination to do what is right for the other person. It is so easy to think that love is being nice. Being loving and compassionate quite often requires you to make a choice for another which they do not have the courage or ability to make. If someone is struggling in their role, then the cruellest thing you can do as a leader is leave them there.

Every day that they are stuck in a position where they don't love, or feel supported, is a day when they take their problems and drudgery back home. It is a day when their family and the world is not getting the best from that individual. It is a day that you are allowing them to waste their life. As a principled leader, can you allow someone to do that? But it is amazingly easy as a leader to ignore. We can get wrapped up in the constant rat race and fail to acknowledge the people in our very teams who are struggling.

Understanding someone well enough so that you can help them does not require you to be their friend or to know their life story. It requires your heart and ears to be open enough that you can hear their problems and distinguish between a bad day and a life that is being lost in the corporate noise. You need to give space for people to be, so that you can pick up on the signals of someone in distress - these signals can be incredibly subtle. It requires you to care for your people as human beings, not as commodities or assets. I hate the line "our greatest assets are our people", no they are not. They are your business; without them nothing would happen. People are not assets to be counted on a spreadsheet, they are to be nurtured and supported, so that they can be the greatest versions of themselves. Anything less, and you are selling them and your business, short.

But as leaders, we must also realise that we are human beings, which means we are not perfect, we will have bad days, there will be people in our teams who push our buttons and potentially irritate us. So how do you balance that with compassionate leadership? How do you manage to authentically hold the space for others if they wind you up?

How do you have those tough conversations from love? You have to actively put yourself in their shoes and you need to leave your ego at the door.

I have a technique that I use in especially tricky cases, where I sit down and write down everything that frustrates me about that individual: Is it their timekeeping? Attitude to junior members of staff or problem customer? The ability to pass the buck, no matter what their job description says? I get it all down on paper, I don't hold back, and then I pause. This process is not about me pulling together an argument for dismissal or anything formal; this technique is me trying to get my subconscious biases out of the way so that I can rationally and lovingly move forward with the conversation I need to have with that individual.

I then write down everything I know about them. Do they have kids? What is their home situation currently like? Are there any stressors I know about that are likely to be impacting their performance?

Then I tend to stand up, take a deep breath and shut my eyes. I picture myself sitting at their desk, in their space. I try to think about how they will be feeling, then pick up what I have written and read it from their perspective. I think about every response they would have to my comments. I align that with what I do know about their current situation, and then, most critically, I think about things I have not asked them recently.

Maybe they have an ill relative who they have to drop to the other side of town every morning, perhaps they are feeling lost and no longer know how to do their job and are feeling threatened by others in the organisation. Maybe they just don't want to be in this role anymore but don't have the courage or know-how to start the conversation at home, let alone with the boss. Whatever it is, I think about their views and write it down. Then, I re-read it.

I then shut my eyes again and feel how I need to proceed. Sometimes, the first thing I do is pick up the phone and just check in on the individual. This process is not about letting poor performance happen, but it is about treating each person as a human being. In my experience, people very, very rarely turn up to work to do a poor job. But they are often in bad places that they don't know how to get out of, or they are looking for more support than they are currently getting. We are too quick to judge others based on our standards and expectations. So, when I take the time to put myself in another's shoes, I know I am giving the respect that I would want.

If I am still feeling frustrated or angry, I always step away, sleep on it, go for a walk and then come back to this again, until I can feel the right path forward.

This method may seem an awful lot of work to deal with someone not operating at their potential, but for me, it ensures that I am approaching the conversation with compassion and respect for the individual holistically, not just as a line on a spreadsheet that is not delivering. It has also been my experience, that often approaching tough conversations differently, changes the outcome. I have seen poor performers change overnight, once they feel listened to and supported. We all want to be heard, we all want to be treated kindly, but we rarely take the time to do that for another. Treat people how you want to be treated is the golden rule for me.

There are some cases where you are not going to change your decision, or you may not be in a position to impact the outcome. Mass redundancies are one of these times, but in these cases, I am now able to engage in a conversation that is based in love, compassion and understanding.

Love allows you to start a discourse based on helping that individual become the best version of themselves. No one sets out in life to be a complete jerk or a bully. Most of the time, people end up there because they are riddled with fear and self-doubt. Acknowledging this, even just to yourself, will give you the patience to deal with any situation, with compassion and grace. Remember, this is not about allowing someone to coast or keeping on people that are no longer needed in your business. Strong leadership is about respecting and loving people enough to show them who they could be and how they should be treated.

It took me time, maturity and a hell of a lot of courage to get to the point where I could dive into another's feelings, and face my own demons about how to lead in conflict. Honestly, I have not walked out of every performance conversation or conflict situation with hugs all around and high fives for great discussions. But, I have walked out knowing that I sat there with them, loved them and engaged in a manner that was founded on compassion and understanding. I have done the best I could on that day. I know it was not just about getting the job done, but doing it in a way that honoured each person in the room. I know it was done by my best self and that is all I can ask of myself, or anyone else.

The Corporate Restructure

There comes the point in all of our careers where we are either having to lead or are impacted at some level by a corporate restructure. Unfortunately, there seems to be a bit of a trend nowadays for the continuous rebuilding of an organisation to make it more streamlined or efficient. Whilst there are a lot of reasons why restructuring is suitable for a business and done well, can reap great rewards, there seems to be a default position at the moment if things aren't working, to return to the drawing board and start again.

I think there are two primary causes:

- Leaders who do not have trust in their decisions - to give them the time to embed and drive the change they initially envisioned. The moment change gets tough (and it always does), leaders fear repercussions and lose faith in themselves. So, they back-pedal or decide to start again. Change needs time, courage and understanding to take place, which requires unwavering leadership. I have seen some examples of this strength, where a leader stuck to their guns, irrespective of the doubters around them, and, in the end, won. If you believe in what you are doing, and the reason for the change, there is no need to second guess yourself constantly;

- Leaders no longer engaging with people as human beings, with lives, experience, ambitions and dreams. It is much easier to move around pieces on a chess board than it is to go and look someone in the eye, to find out why your latest strategy is not working. Disengaging as a leader can feel safer. The impact that your choices can have on people's lives can be significant. They have mortgages to pay and kids to feed, so removing the human factor removes the guilt, I get it.

Yes, every change in business comes with tough decisions, and often decisions that, on a human level, we don't like. But it is far more common for people to step away from the human element and hope that, by building the right set of boxes on an Org Chart, that a miracle will happen and their business will head back to double-digit growth overnight.

What do you do as a leader when you know your company is no longer able to operate in the way it always has, but you want to change with compassion and integrity?

Firstly, you have to start with your people. These are the individuals on the ground who engage on a daily basis with your customers, your product and your suppliers. You want them to change? Well, you better well understand them and their world. It is only through a thorough understanding of your business, as it is today, that you will know what you can and could change, to make it the business you want in the future. Yes, there are consultants out there who can help you, but unless you know your people and what makes them tick, they will be a waste of money.

The need for a business to change usually comes down to increased levels of complexity within the organisation and its processes. Complexity means layers and opaqueness. No matter how approachable or kind you are, as a senior leader, you do not know what it is like at the coalface unless you consciously spend time there, on a regular basis. When was the last time you handled a cold call? When did you last box up your product for shipping? When was the last time you ate your packed lunch in the canteen with everyone else? Compassion starts with a desire to understand and connect with human beings - connect with their hearts. This connection will then allow you to understand the complexity as they see it. You will be able to see your company through their eyes, and this insight will dramatically change your perspective.

True complexity is rarely needed, but has been created out of lack of investment in processes and systems that are fit for purpose, for the future, and from a lack of understanding about why things happen. The problem comes from the fact that getting process and systems in place correctly takes time and significant effort, which usually delays return on investment and is therefore rushed, and complexity arises, as workarounds and bodges are put in place. Get to understand what your people do and their real pain points. Then be willing to assign teams and resources to implement appropriate solutions properly which often removes complexity. Leaders are too quick to want to drive change before they understand the reason for the current state. Yes, organic change can lead to messy processes, as can poor merger strategies and a host of other things. But people rarely make their lives more difficult for the sheer sake of it. If a process is overly complex, there is usually a reason why and you need to understand that first, before you can jump in and solve the problem.

Your people are the heartbeat of the company. You have to connect to them before you can know where the company is and how the company is feeling. You have to understand why they do what they do.

In reality, speed of action and return to growth, encourages leaders to leapfrog the step of connecting in with their company's heartbeat, but this is to the peril of the success of long-term change and improvement. We are judged and measured on how quickly we can do things, but we seem to have lost respect for doing this thoroughly and correctly. Fast, loses people, and what feels slow to you, will still feel very quick to a majority of your people. With speed we lose connection, we lose creativity, and we lose the very essence that makes us unique.

I ask, as you start to look at changing your organisation, that you take time and compassion, for the process to happen correctly. Whole industries are now so caught up in the rhythm of constant change that they have stalled. We have sacrificed creativity and innovation for speed and action, and, as a consequence, we have lost. No success can come from speed and action alone.

How does your organisation breathe? It may seem like a strange question, and it is, but consider your own breath. As you start to become conscious of the way you breathe, there are times when you notice that your breath is shallow and fast. There are times when your breath is slow and deep. It is very easy to correlate your breath to your state and your emotions. When stressed or distracted, we tend to breathe more shallowly and quite quickly, not allowing our bodies to fully make use of the precious oxygen that it needs to thrive and operative at its most efficient. When we are breathing slowly and deeply, we are usually in a more relaxed and calmer state, able to have rational thoughts and make decisions that are considered and balanced.

So how is your organisation breathing? My guess, as I have seen this many times, is that your company's breath is quick and shallow. It is stressed, unsure what is coming next, and unable to really sit back and make balanced, rational decisions. This means your people are distracted and not operating at their most productive. What can you do to help the breath of the company change?

Just as we learn any new skill or habit, it takes time for it to embed itself in our daily practice and we need constant reminders to ensure that, over time, it becomes a natural part of our day. As a leader who wants to take an organisation through change, you have to be the cue to your team to become aware of where you are and take a deep breath or two. This can either be an actual reminder to take a breather, or even just a regular acknowledgement of where you are as a team and what you have achieved to date.

I work with companies all over the globe to support them in implementing organisational change, and the three key take-away's from all of the experiences I have had are:

1. Slow down - no change is so urgent that it has to be done today. Most changes I have seen have been driven by external factors, so there is an assumption that the change must happen. It is rare that organisations take the time to consider if a change is right for them and their

strategy. Take the time to reflect on all of the aspects of change. This also gives you the time to get your reason for change tested. Don't change for change's sake; it is a waste of time and energy;

2. Breathe, check in with yourself and your teams. How are they breathing? Trying to convince anyone to do anything on top of their day job is hard enough, but to do that during times of stress gets much tougher. Make sure your organisation is in a good place before you dive headfirst into change;

3. Commit to change at their speed. We often drive change from the top, but that means we have pondered this for much longer than layers further down the organisation. Give respect to each member of your staff to accept and acknowledge change at their pace. Pushing people will only create resistance and lack of engagement.

Before you embark on any organisational restructure, give yourself the chance as a leader to get to know how your company feels. Then, use that to guide you through implementing any changes if truly needed.

• • •

Lesson: Love and patience will help you to resolve any conflict and will guide you on how to act.

Everybody deserves to be treated with love and respect. This is a sign of strength as a leader, so use it to understand your business and the needs of each of the people who work for you.

- Don't shy away from conflict but use it as an opportunity to learn and support each other;

- In a tough conversation ask questions, wait to give your opinion. Don't assume just because you are higher up the hierarchy that you know best;

- Listen, you were born with two ears and one mouth, use them in that ratio!

- Trust yourself, once you have all of the information and you have made the decision that feels right, stick it out and don't waiver to please others.

CORPORATE LOVE

I was recently told to put my finger in a glass of water and then remove it. My wise companion then asked me where the hole I left was. Laughing, I said there isn't one, which was his point exactly. Individuals in corporations are like fingers in water - when they leave, the hole doesn't exist.

Our corporate culture is in a race to the bottom. We have removed all ability for people to bring their personal values to work. Instead, we demand presence and 24/7 availability in a race to drive our workforce into mindless zombies. Fewer and fewer people jump out of bed in the morning filled with joy at the prospect of how they are going to pass the day. Instead, we spend hours responding to email after email or dialling into back to back video conferences. The statistics about how this is both affecting our economy and our health are staggering. Stress is quickly becoming the number one killer in the western world, and our lack of productivity is increasing.

According to a Gallup State of the Global Workplace report, only 15% of the global workforce is engaged. That is a statistic that would make any leader question how they are leading their teams and where the focus is. Yes, I believe your customer is important, but we know far more about our customers than we generally do about our own employees. I think our focus needs to be on the people that dedicate their time every working day to our companies. If we put them first and make them feel valued and celebrated for what they do, they, in turn, will look after our customers with joy.

We have created barren environments where expressions of creativity and self-expression are segmented off to specialist "innovation" departments in a clear message that states "we don't want you to think or feel".

This, combined with an education system in most countries, which is designed to remove creativity from children, and force them to learn a curriculum that is neither fit for purpose any more nor able to adequately prepare them to be citizens that can drive change in our societies, is forcing us into a scary situation where the "haves" and the "have-nots" are drifting further and further apart. We are creating a perfect storm of disillusion, where millions of people feel that they are unable to contribute meaningfully and cannot see a place for themselves in the world.

Talk to a millennial, and in most cases, they are struggling to understand how they can relate to the world that the generations before them have created. The competition for good-paying jobs is insane, the level of debt that our higher education system burdens them with from such a young age is a lead weight that will follow them through a significant portion of their adult life, and then we are forcing them into a corporate culture that only pays lip-service to understanding them but really just wants them to conform.

Imagine a place of work filled with laughter and joy. A workplace where the employee comes first, not the bottom line. With engaged, excited employees who can easily articulate the value your products and services delivered to their customers, looking to deliver excellence in service because they love what they do. For many, this is just a pipe dream, but it is my belief that without changing our organisational culture to one based on love, we are in a very fast descent into corporate oblivion. We cannot carry on expecting our staff to show up to work and be productive members of society if we give them an environment meant for conformity.

In rare cases, colleagues become real friends, but often these relationships are formed in the united whinging about their circumstances. At what point did we start to believe that spending eight to 10 hours of our days in misery or ambivalence was acceptable?

It may seem very simplistic, but I believe by supporting our staff to begin to love not only themselves but their roles, their customers and their lives, that we can rebuild our company culture. Love unites, love creates, and love thrives. Contrast that to how most large businesses are existing at the moment.

In the last section of this book, I will outline how you can start rebuilding the culture within your company, no matter where you are in the hierarchy - helping you understanding how you can be a catalyst for significant and impactful change through stepping into a role that we are all designed to excel at.

I have created a number of exercises and frameworks that can be used individually or sequentially, in workshops or team meetings, to pull team members together and forge the bonds needed to thrive in their work and support of each other.

Example 1 - What happens if one of my team is not responding to my leadership style?

There are times when no matter what you do or how safe an environment you create, a team member will not engage. They either don't see value in what you are trying to build or they are not comfortable to open up and be vulnerable with either you or a team member.

The first question you need to answer must be: Is this person disengaged from their role and the team?

There is a big difference between being disengaged and being unable to engage as part of the team. There are some people who, no matter what you do, will never feel comfortable speaking out, and that is OK, as long as they are doing the job they need to do for you and the rest of the team. If this is the case, it is important that you and the team acknowledge this and that you check in with each other to ensure you are supporting a very introverted team member. However, if they are actively disengaged and undermining the team, then you need to deal with the situation quickly.

Everyone in a team has a job to do, but not everyone needs to be ambitious or have high-potential. We need diversity of passions, talents, capabilities and desires within a team to make it successful. Not everyone needs or wants to be in the spotlight. Think of an operating theatre; each individual has their own unique, and critical, role to perform: the surgeon, the anaesthetist, the nurses, the porters, and the cleaners, etc. Without each person, the possibility of success changes dramatically, and yet only one or two can be the star surgeons. High-performing teams are like this. Everyone needs to know their role and the value that it adds to the team.

Disengaged team members can actively and quickly disrupt any new team dynamic and they are most likely not doing the job that the team needs. This is when you need to ensure that you can have an honest conversation about what you and the team need from this individual. If they are not willing to deliver, then you need to openly and honestly formulate a plan.

Always acknowledge that you are not a trained counsellor and if people have issues that are beyond your skills, then get them professional help if you can. Your role is to make your team as successful and as high-performing as possible, but realise you cannot be the perfect leader for everyone.

Any leader worth their salt already knows that you have to tweak your leadership style to a degree with each member of the team, but this should not mean that you become a different person. You need to maintain style consistency so that the team can recognise you and your behaviours in all situations.

So, determine if your team member is not participating but committed to the team. If yes, then openly decide as a team if this is acceptable and if this supports the objectives you are all trying to achieve. Remember, successful teams need diversity. If you decide you have a team member who is disengaged, then you need to work with them to rediscover their passion and that may not be within your team. For the success of you and your team, do this quickly.

• • •

I have been fortunate that for the majority of my career I have worked in both an industry and a role that I love. Working in the education industry has allowed me to feel fulfilled by what I do, as I can see the impact I am having. Whilst working in sales has allowed me to work directly with our customers to solve their problems. More often than not, those solutions lead to people being able to reach their potential, whether it is improving access to education through technology, the quality of learning through teacher professional development or access to higher education pathways that open doors that were otherwise shut, I have had a career that has had an impact on lives. And that is the highest honour.

However, I have also spent a lot of my career surrounded by people going through the motions, turning up to work to pay the mortgage. If they are lucky enough to enjoy what they do, they are still not driven by passion or love. This situation has to change. The impact of a disenfranchised workforce is significant to our economy, and our health and it is only going to get worse unless we face some hard truths.

We cannot, and must not, treat people as a commodity or assets. We have to treat them as beings, human beings, and that means creating an environment that allows them to thrive and be creative.

For those of you gifted to be parents, you will know that you deliberated and researched your choice of childcare provider, nursery and school. It had to be an environment that you know would suit your most precious offspring and one in which they would reach their potential. It had to nurture; it had to excite; it had to allow for creativity and be filled with people who would offer your children love, attention and support.

This type of environment is what we need to create in our workplaces.

I regularly hear that complexity is killing sustainable growth in businesses and whilst I cannot dispute that this is true, I think the root cause of this complexity is more straightforward than many people make it out to be.

When you start a company, you do it for love, for the love of helping the customer, for the love of your great product, for the sheer joy of having the freedom to be you and do what you love. No one creates a company from hate or ambivalence.

As companies grow and become successful, you stop being able to focus on what you love and you focus on the tasks that you should or have to do. This is where we start going wrong.

Complexity is not due to the size or speed of growth; it is down to a lack of connection between the people in a company. It is down to the lack of love between your company, your product, your customer and your people.

What is currently the biggest complaint in your company? It is usually the lack of sustainable growth. Why are you not growing? The answer is scarily simple - your people don't love what they do. If your people were in love with their jobs, they would create products and services that would thrill; they would sing about what you do with such passion that people would be queuing up to place orders.

At your next team meeting, don't ask people what they are going to do. Ask them why they came to work this morning. If the answer does not fill your heart with joy, then you have some work to do. And be clear, it is not their fault. You, as a leader, have allowed a culture and environment to grow that doesn't encourage and praise loving what you do. How do you act as a leader? Are you filled with passion for your customers and compassion for your team? If you're not, then that is the first place to start. You need to be a beacon of joy as many days as is humanly possible (remember, we are humans and thus, not perfect!)

By finding the joy in what we do, we can start to remove the complexity that is so commonly blamed for increased bureaucracy and slowing growth in many companies. I mentioned earlier in this book that I had, many times, confused complexity with hard. I think this is often the case in a corporate environment. It is hard and takes time to makes sure that as a leader you know precisely what you need your people to be doing and that you take the time to hire the right person with the right attitude and dreams to do each job. It is then even more laborious and time-consuming to develop each of those people and as a team to continue to grow, develop and deepen their love for what they do. So we avoid the detail. The moment we avoid the detail, the situation looks complex and messy and even less attractive to pour your energy into.

During one of the retreats I did to a Buddhist monastery in France, I cleaned out the lotus pond. It just so happened that it was pouring it down with rain and we were all knee deep in mud. One of my fellow visitors asked a nun why we had to do this, as we pulled wheelbarrow after wheelbarrow of dirt, old lotus roots and leaves out of the lake. The nun simply responded by saying that if the lotus roots weren't clean then the flowers would never bloom as beautifully as they could.

Getting too stuck in the weeds is something that I have been told leaders should avoid, but to me, that is the critical piece of leading a team successfully. You must understand how clean the roots are to know how well your flower is going to bloom. But it is a mucky job that is undesirable and requires effort.

I learn what my team does - I don't have to know every detail, nor do I have to do the tasks for them, but I need to know what the mud and the dead leaves are so that I can help clear them away. Interestingly, what I find most often is that the "mud" is rarely the process or the actual tasks themselves, but it is the environment in which they occur. If your staff don't feel praised or valued, they will not be in the right state of mind to deliver to their full potential. Whilst it is critical that we get companies set up in a way that processes and supporting systems are seamless, the first step has to be creating an environment that lets the individual employee bloom.

IT STARTS WITH YOU

Change starts with you as a leader. I have worked in many different types of companies, small start-ups all the way through to some big global corporate brands, and emotional support is not something I think I have ever really experienced until recently. As leaders, we are expected to be authentic in a way that is very confined and dignified. We are not allowed to express ourselves fully, lest we become seen as unstable. The question "How are you?" is not something that we are permitted to answer honestly, just in case we destabilise the trust of the business. But the truth is that human beings cannot be inspiring and motivating all the time. We cannot be on our 'A' game 24/7, and we cannot always be right in our choices.

I had grown up in the corporate world to feel that at work I had to be in control and upbeat. At home, I am what I am. There are days when I am so nauseatingly optimistic and bouncy that my kids want to lock me in the bedroom until I calm down, and there are days when I don't really want to engage with anyone. But you cannot be that as a leader, or so I thought. How we show up and act is our choice. I know I can, on a down day, be inspiring and do what has to be done. Somehow you tap into that well of energy that will make you go the extra mile. But you cannot do it all the time. You come across as fake.

Hearing this, for me, was a huge shock when it was first fed back to me. I honestly thought that by putting on my game face and being what I thought a leader was every day, I was doing what I should. What I discovered, was that I was being experienced in a completely different way. People felt that I could not be vulnerable, that I was intimidating, that I was not approachable and that I would not understand them. My wish to show up as inspiring and motivating all the time was actually pushing people away. They wanted to see the chinks in my armour.

The reality is that I don't think many people really know me. I don't share my fears or my dreams with many, and that means that any real deep connection is rare. I have always said that I would tell anyone anything, that I have nothing to hide, but that allows me to hide behind the reality that no one will ask. You don't ask people the tough or probing questions. No wonder I have come across as fake or inauthentic at times.

As I started to prepare to write this book, I decided that I needed to poke and push every trigger or button that I may have. Opening yourself up for the first time in published print is a ballsy thing to do, I knew nothing was going to stop me from doing it, but I had to be writing from a place of truth. I could not let my ego publish a book about love to gain admiration. Instead, I had to prepare my soul to write and deal with the inevitable criticism and potential hate. I had to get to the point where I did not care how this was received, but that I was strong enough to acknowledge, firstly to myself and then to others, what I had never told anyone before.

I didn't know where to start. How do you learn to be vulnerable and authentic? Was there a LinkedIn course I could do? What if I couldn't let my masks go? So I started looking around, trying to find leaders that I could emulate or compare myself to. I was trying to make this easy.

But luckily, as always, the universe delivered exactly what I needed. It was hard and messy but mercifully fast.

Example 2 - How do you build your own faith in your team?

When you first step in as a new leader, building trust with your team and your peers has to be a priority. But this is not always as simple as it may seem. You can guarantee that there will be a backstory that you may not know, or a political land mine that you may (probably will) stand on. Beware of the "First 100 days" syndrome. It is very common for a new person entering an organisation to bounce in, filled with enthusiasm and new ideas, and try to drive change from day one. But there is often a reason something has not been tried or implemented that you have seen work elsewhere.

My recipe is Listen, Observe, Learn, Suggest. People will rarely trust someone who doesn't know context or dictates a solution. Give yourself a timeline, for example three months, to just listen and learn your team, the company and the market. Be open about this with all of your stakeholders so you are setting the right expectations. This will give you time to overcome any preconceived ideas about the role or the market, as well as allowing you time to gather as much 360-degree insight as you can. Do this even if you have been promoted from within. You probably know less than you think.

Let you team carry on as normal, they know what they are doing. Once you have reached the end of your timeline, sit down with your team and share your observations as a group. Remember, you should talk last. Then, together, build your strategy and then implement it decisively.

Giving your team time also allows you to empower existing leaders. As a leader, I like to get to know the entirety of my team, not just my direct reports, but this can be problematic if you don't approach it mindfully. The last thing you want to do is disempower your existing team managers by overriding what they say or how they lead. By stepping back, listening and learning, you will lay the foundations for future success.

The ego aims to separate you from others, forcing you to hold back, not display your emotions and conform to what our society thinks as normal. The more we connect with ourselves and others, the more scared and reactive the ego gets. I had this happen to me again recently. I met someone new who I immediately knew and trusted. I did not know why or how, but this was someone who I felt I had loved for a long time and I knew I was safe with them and could fully be myself. This scared the crap out of me, or I should say, my ego. I became guarded, I listened, but didn't share. I held back when I should have pushed them to be their best self, and I held back from communicating with them because I was scared of the connection to this person.

The depth of this friendship scared me. But people come into our lives for a reason, they are here to teach us to become better versions of ourselves, and I knew deep down that this person was there not only to push me but for me to support and make them thrive. Some stay for a long time, others are fleeting, and I had no idea which type this friendship was. For me, holding back was not helping either of us.

I knew this person had been brought into my life to teach me how to open up and trust another and, therefore, learn to be vulnerable. It was not only a skill I had to learn, but a guard I had to drop.

But my brain kept telling me that it was not sensible to trust someone you barely knew and had only met a couple of times. But my heart was screaming at me that I was safe and I could trust, but having spent so much of my time in my head, it is still not always easy to ignore my brain. Luckily, I am surrounded by wise friends, and one of them told me that by holding back, I was hurting both of us. This is what the ego does. It hurts us by stopping us connecting and learning from each other. It separates us in order to make us feel nervous, unsafe and fearful so that we don't act when we know we should.

It took me a couple of days to pluck up the courage to have the conversation I needed to have with this individual, but I am immensely glad I did. Love is what binds us together and comes in many shapes and sizes; we must embrace it, not run from it or fear it.

Opening up just once to tell someone why I had acted in the way I had was the first step. The next was doing this again, but in a situation that required me to be the bravest I have ever been.

Coming off the back of a week-long work trip, I was exhausted, and it was another long week on the road with a full leadership team day on the Wednesday, which I was dreading. We had a whole day, as a team, giving and receiving feedback on each other. I had done numerous days like this before, and they had never bothered me, in fact, I usually loved the opportunity to engage with my peers in a new way. But tiredness and a more profound understanding of my lack of trust and ability to be vulnerable, was leaving me in a delicate state. I did not feel safe, emotionally.

It didn't take long for the terror to rise and the overwhelming sense that I was not safe in the room to have me crying my heart out in the nearest toilet.

Somehow, I had the courage to stay in the room, and I openly wept in front of all my peers and my boss. I couldn't have held it back if I had tried. I did not feel safe, and I did not feel safe being me. I eventually blurted out to the room what I was feeling, and I let go.

I let go of my mask. I have been brought up in corporate cultures where I have been told over and over again that I am great, I am a natural-born leader and I am one of the best. I have had companies invest significant amounts of money in my development, and I had believed that at work I am significantly better than most at what I do. I think I believed that that made be a better person. That week, that belief finally (and luckily), came tumbling down. I have long held the notion that I am no better or no worse than any other person on this planet, but in the workplace, my ego has put up an incredible fight to ensure that is not the case.

At work, I have been better than others and I had progressed quickly, and so my ego has built up the roles and masks to allow me to stand there with my shoulders back in front of a packed room and know that I own it. In most companies, it works. The stronger your mask, the better they think you are and don't for a second try and dislodge yours or anyone else's, as the house of cards may well crumble around everyone. But we need to be different if we are going to reverse the trend of increased employee disengagement and decreasing productivity.

This facade that we protect is not supporting us, and it was not protecting me in any way, it was just delaying the impact and the lesson I needed to learn in order to grow. We need to accept that what we have traditionally valued in the workplace no longer nourishes those around us, and we need to acknowledge that we have to change as leaders.

Trying to be more vulnerable and authentic is teaching me lessons I need to learn, and it has allowed me to connect with some amazing human beings in a way I never have before. I can honestly say that I felt like I was being emotionally hung, drawn and quartered every day. I felt as though I was being broken down, piece by piece, and I had to learn how to put myself back together. I have never been more grateful for the opportunity to have changed so much in such a short space of time.

For some, this ability of opening up comes naturally, but for many of us, it requires time and a commitment to psych ourselves up and take the plunge into trusting others as we have never done before. We have to put faith in the fact that there will be more people who love us afterwards than hate us, and we have to believe that we are building connections that will allow us to bring more love and joy into our lives.

I am still not very good at opening myself up and being vulnerable, but being aware has made me understand how much I have held myself back from people. That is something that I am not willing to do anymore. I talk and live through love, and that means letting people close to me see me as I am, not how I want them to.

Next, I needed to work out how I pulled this all together, to find out what truly makes me a good and authentic leader. I have always been an OK leader, I naturally have thought it best to put my people as my main focus, and I know what excites me, what makes me work every hour, I know what makes me proud, I know how it feels to love, but I wanted to distil this into something I could share.

My list of fears was pretty long, and these seemed to be the main reason why I was not holding back from letting myself be an authentic leader. I am sharing a few of them with you now, but

I have never shared these openly before. I suspect that anyone with kids has some similar fears, but I wouldn't know, because I was never brave enough to have that conversation with anyone.

I am sharing these as we have to lead by example, we can't ask our teams to do or be anything that we are not willing to. To be genuinely authentic, I have to be an open book to those who I am asking to trust me. It is easy sometimes to share for reaction or pity. I know I have been guilty of that in the past, but sharing what your deepest truth is, opens you up. It allows others to see depth and vulnerability that we otherwise hide. Sharing builds connection. But it requires bravery and strength.

- What if I let my kids down?

- What if I fail?

- What if I fuck up my relationship with my other half because of my career, again? (I did!)

- What if I am not successful?

- What if I am not as good as I think I am?

- What if I stop holding back, open myself up and people attack me for it?

- What if I get found out that I am not as good as I think I am or pretend to be?

- What if, what if, what if…?

You get the gist. All these fears that race around our heads. For me, they got louder and louder the more senior I got and the bigger the team I led.

In a way, dealing with each one of these was easy, I had the skills in tapping and meditation to work through them one by one, but the driver I had to find was my "Why?" What was motivating and driving me to do all this work on myself to make myself a better leader?

HOW TO BE VULNERABLE

Vulnerability is a skill you have to learn as it is contrary to our natural instincts to protect ourselves. We have survived as a species because we have become experts at protecting ourselves, from the elements, from physical hardship and from emotional pain. But it is these layers of protection that stop us from being vulnerable, to opening up completely to those around us. Like many ideas that have gained significant popularity over the last few years, the concept of vulnerability is far easier to buy into than the reality. It feels right, but it is much harder to put into practice.

Learning to notice the difference between our rational and irrational fears, emotionally, gives us the power to choose how we act in the face of these fears. It is completely rational to be afraid of falling off a cliff, it is irrational if that fear stops you from ever getting in an elevator. It is these irrational fears that often stop us from opening up emotionally.

Vulnerability is spoken about as if it is as simple as flipping the switch to turn on. But for most of us, we have been conditioned from childhood not to truly express ourselves or how we feel. Being able to be completely vulnerable requires us to know, with every cell in our bodies that, no matter what, we are loved.

As leaders, we are usually used to being praised or getting adulation, but that is often our ego or fear driving us to seek validation of who we are and how we are perceived by others. The current corporate environment and many leadership programmes are unlikely to breed vulnerability, and that is why true vulnerability or authenticity is so often missing in our leaders today. In fact, the majority of the training I have been given has encouraged me to be anything but truly vulnerable, whilst still appearing authentic, a feat that is impossible.

Standing on a stage to speak or lead others takes guts. For many, it requires overcoming deep-seated fears, the way that we are coached to deal with these situations is to put on your game face. We are told to step up, to just get on with it, and that means putting on a mask, playing a role. The moment you accept a role to play, you cannot be vulnerable or authentic. That mask protects us and allows us to push through our fears, but if we cannot drop the facade and let our true selves shine through, it becomes another layer of protection, another way of disconnecting us from people.

We talk about vulnerability in our leaders and the work place, but what does that actually mean. How do we teach people to be vulnerable? How do we make it safe for people to feel that they can open up?

Through a lot of research, in leading and in working on myself, I have seen that there are three key stages to becoming truly vulnerable. Whilst the simplicity of that may sound enticing, the hard work and willingness to let go of control as a leader is not for the faint-hearted. But it is worth the effort, not only for your own happiness, but also to allow you to achieve the goals that you are aiming for with your teams.

I think it is worth stating that being vulnerable does not mean that you are an emotional mess all the time. We seem to think that vulnerability is only about expressing our deepest feelings, that in some way it is only about showing our weaknesses. But true vulnerability is the willingness to be the you that you are at that moment, without any filter or mask. Sometimes that will be playful, serious, emotional, sensitive, determined, or a mix of all the emotions that we experience on a daily basis. It is about being real. Being vulnerable means accepting and expressing both the strengths and the weaknesses of who you are and not apologising for them.

Below are the three stages of becoming vulnerable:

1. Recognise, embrace and release your fears;

2. Let go of controlling the outcome;

3. Build a plan of how to deal with constant knocks - as they are going to come!

Each of these steps involved courage to dig deep and examine myself and my behaviours. Below, I have detailed how I went through each of these stages, and this is exactly how I teach others to do the same.

As with everything in this book, I ask that you are patient and kind with yourself and others, and know that the speed in which people will go through this process will be unique to the individual. You cannot schedule personal growth and you may even find that some members of your team are not ready to make such a step, and that is something that you will have to accept, difficult and frustrating as that might be.

Learning to be Vulnerable

The ability to be vulnerable, for me, has started with building the unshakeable belief in myself that I am safe. No matter how logically I understood that my physical safety could not be affected by the outcome of my openness, I could not still the fear that arose in my stomach each time I knew I was going to have to be vulnerable. Vulnerability required me to let go of the outcome, I could not dictate how someone would react to me, or what I said. But I could ensure that I was being 100% me in the moment.

1. Recognise, embrace and release your fears;

2. Let go of controlling the outcome;

3. Build a plan of how to deal with constant knocks - as they are going to come!

Recognise, Embrace and Release Your Fears

Even if you were born into the most loving and supportive environment, you will have picked up negative and limiting beliefs about yourself during childhood and adolescence that will have separated you from the belief that you are loveable. You will have built your layers of protection from emotional pain, and you will have made assumptions about yourself and a situation, sometimes without all the facts.

Bear with me if I start to get a bit new age here, but we are all born pure and carefree. As we develop and start to understand that we are both part of this world and yet an individual within it, we build constructs and beliefs about how we should interact, be and show up, and we create our roles and our masks. This is normal, and if you are lucky enough to be good at what you do in a corporate environment, certain beliefs about yourself are accentuated, whilst you will be allowed to hide from others.

The rise of strengths-based leadership and development was a great step forward, but it let us step even further away from vulnerability. We were asked to only focus on our strengths and attributes that make us successful. Although there is a lot of sense in getting better at what you are naturally good at, it gave us the opportunity to ignore our natural weaknesses and gave us a reason not to be vulnerable. It gave us a green light to hide behind our strengths.

As a leader, or an inspiring leader, you may well have heard that you are bright, or clever, that you have natural leadership skills, that you are driven, ambitious, high achieving. But all of these labels slowly become a belief system. They become how we think we should act to carry on being successful. They start to make us step away from being open and vulnerable, as they become a benchmark, against which we start to measure ourselves and our actions, instead of letting our undeniable and loving strength of who we truly are, lead us.

The belief system that you build around your work persona or mask becomes stronger as these beliefs are supported by others, yet they often run contrary to the beliefs that we have created in childhood, so we have this dichotomy of rising through the corporate ranks and, yet, at the same time, feeling that we are about to be found out for the fraud that we are; the well-known Imposter Syndrome.

This syndrome has been created by the battle in our heads between our different masks and belief systems. Until we can create peace, pull the belief systems together and release any limiting beliefs, we will constantly be in the state of high alert, feeling that we are about to be unveiled as an imposter.

The rate of change within the workplace has got faster and faster which means that this battle is raging more ferociously than ever before, as the contrast between what we believe about ourselves and what we need to be to succeed becomes starker.

This increase in speed has also made it tougher to create the trust that we know is a critical ingredient for any successful leader. Trust takes time to create, and the only way to speed up the organic creation of trust is to let go of the outdated methods of gung-ho "rally the troops" type leadership and connect with people on a much deeper level, so that they can leap before they understand, as they know that you will be there to support them every step of the journey.

As this is a book about team building and leadership, I will be focusing on that, but there are many great books which examine this concept in a wider setting. The techniques described in this book are equally applicable outside the workplace.

In the last chapter, we looked at the list of my fears that have run around my head and separated me from others and myself. Now it is time for you to look at yours.

We need to recognise our fears before we can embrace and release them.

Exercise - Listing your limiting beliefs

Find a quiet spot where you won't be disturbed for at least 10 minutes. Have a pen and paper. There are notes pages at the back of this book for you to use.

Take five deep breaths, counting to four on the inhale and six on the exhale.

Now you have calmed your body and your mind, I want you to slowly answer the following questions:

What is holding you back from sharing yourself completely with your team?

Answers may appear such as: I don't want to look like a fool; they work for me; what does it matter; I'm not as good as people think I am. Or you may experience resistance, which usually looks like: This is stupid; I'm not scared, etc. This resistance is fear; fear of you looking at who you are and what you could be. This is natural and OK, but recognise it for what it is.

Write down everything that comes up for you, don't rush this process.

Why do I think I am holding myself back?

Answers may be: I don't know how people are going to react; I am worried I will be judged; What will people think of me?; I'm scared of being hurt again; What if I fail? Remember, no matter how hard we try to separate our work lives from our home lives, our belief system was created in our childhood and re-enforced throughout our lives, so our personal experience will impact how we react at work.

Write down everything that comes up for you, don't rush this process.

What do I really believe about myself?

This is a tricky one to answer sometimes, as our ego immediately wants to protect us. But give yourself some time, take a few more deep breaths, and the answers will come. Please don't be surprised if the answers are not pretty, at this stage they are not meant to be. I can guarantee that most of the beliefs you have about yourself you inherited or heard from someone else.

Typical answers to this question are: People will laugh at me; I'll be judged; I'm not loveable; I don't deserve love; I'm not good enough; I have to be perfect.

Write down everything that comes up for you, don't rush this process.

I recommend doing this process two or three times over the space of a week. Unless you are used to self-inquiry, asking yourself probing questions such as these, will feel unnatural, so give yourself time. You can also revisit this process again and again. As I discuss in stage three, becoming and staying vulnerable is not a one-time thing, it is a process that you will do over and over again.

The next step is to embrace these beliefs. I know that sounds weird, but it you don't accept these beliefs you cannot change them and let them go. The more we fight something, the harder it is for us to change. These beliefs are rarely a choice we have consciously made, the majority of our beliefs are not even ours, but have been handed down to us through our upbringing. Any negative beliefs we hold about ourselves are not our fault, but it is our responsibility to acknowledge them, and then let them go if we want to grow as leaders.

Each new belief I uncovered felt different. Sometimes, my reaction was to want to push back and refuse to accept that I was being driven by something so wrong. Other times, I needed to sit with a belief to understand its impact, and then there were the times when I point bank refused to acknowledge I believed such a thing about myself. But the process of embracing a belief, as is, starts the healing, and allows you to start to let your sub-conscious know that you can let this belief go.

Beliefs are strange things, they are both a conscious and sub-conscious choice, so we need to treat them as such. Embracing them brings them into our consciousness and that is the first step in allowing us to change them.

I use tapping to clear my beliefs. It is the most effective and quickest way I have found. I will sit down with my list and score each limiting belief on a scale of zero to 10, zero being I don't believe this at all, through to 10 being I believe this with every cell in my body. I then tap through the points until I feel the belief being let go. Once I have felt the belief go, I continue to tap, but this time saying the belief that I want to take its place.

For example, when working through the belief that I did not deserve to be loved, I let it go and then spent about three minutes tapping in the belief - "I am loveable and I deserve to be loved". Whilst tapping may seem simplistic, it is immensely powerful and transformative.

On my website www.helenhonisett.com there are a number of tapping scripts that I have created to help you through this process. Feel free to change these so that they are right for you, but scripts are a great way to start if you are new to tapping.

Tapping works for me, but I acknowledge it won't be for everyone, I encourage you to give it a go. However, if you do find another technique that works for you, please let me know.

Letting Go of the Outcome

The concept of control is a minefield for a leader. Leaders are meant to be in control. We are supposed to be able to control our teams, our actions and the outcome. How else are we going to hit our targets?

The concept of letting go of the outcome immediately puts most leaders out of their comfort zone. But to be truly vulnerable, that is exactly what we have to do. I am not saying let go of strategy, planning and your destination. It is critical you know these so you can take your people there. But how you get there will change - you need to let go of the how.

You cannot control the future; you cannot control people's reaction to you, and you cannot control the result. All you can do is be the best person you can be in any given moment. All you can control is who you are.

So, why waste your precious energy doing anything else?

This was the hardest lesson I had to learn. Not only had I spent decades priding myself on my ability to be a control freak, I had used this as a skill to ensure I was successful. I tried to control everything I could so that I could ensure that my goals were going to be achieved. I was taught to do this, and in sales, it is seen as critical skill. I knew every step on the path – well, I thought I did.

I spent hours in conversation with myself going through all the combinations and permutations of any action, I would over-think any interaction with another to make sure I could understand how they would respond. I would worry about everything, my mind would race with what-ifs and if-only's to the point of distraction and often sleeplessness.

But all this energy was being wasted and I was adding significant stress to my life, as well as adrenaline and cortisol to my body.

I am not saying don't care about the outcome, I am not saying stop making goals and aim for something incredible. But you do need to acknowledge and understand that the only thing you have any power over is yourself. Focus all your energy on constantly being the best you can be, and you will be able to hit every target you can ever set for yourself.

But most of us spend too much time worrying about how people will respond, or trying to fix the conditions in some way, when that is something we need to relinquish.

The moment that you are able to be vulnerable will be scary, not only for you, but for others around you. How they react will be based on their own fears and beliefs. There is nothing you can do about it, but be there to love and support them and yourself. I have had people walk away from me, cry on me and call me a whole host of names when I have opened up and spoken from a place of vulnerability. I have also had people cheer me on, respond in kind and talk to me in a way I never thought possible. That is the risk, and the reward, that you have to take. It is the risk that every leader needs to be willing to take, to build strong, united teams. A leader must be willing to risk all for the people they work with.

Like many things, our obsession with control comes from fear, often a fear of being judged and being found out. Identifying these fears and using tapping to let them go has allowed me to release my grip on controlling every aspect of my life and the people in it.

It is an on-going process, but one that I know has made a significant difference not only to my ability to lead openly, but also my productivity, as I now focus my energy solely on what I need to be doing, rather than wasting it on controlling others.

Exercise - What's the best that could happen?

Do you worry too much? Do you overthink situations? Do you expect the worst in any circumstance? Then you are too vested in the outcome.

It has taken me time to come to peace about the outcome. Que sera, sera is a state of mind that takes discipline to cultivate but it has been worth the work, as I can now focus all of my energy on my goals and dreams.

Tapping and meditation are a great way to remove deep rooted anxiety and to find peace, but early on in my journey I found this exercise beneficial to balance the constant worry in my head. I spent so much time focusing on the negative outcome that I never paid any attention to the positive. But giving myself the space to think about both sides of the equation, I started to gain perspective, and therefore, a more balanced view and approach to any situation that was causing me stress.

- Take a piece of paper and at the top of the page write "What's the best that can happen?"

- Underneath this heading, write a very brief synopsis of the situation or issue that is causing you stress or anxiety;

- Now spend –five to 10 minutes listing all the positive outcomes that could happen in this situation. For example, if you are about to have an appraisal conversation with one of your team who are underperforming slightly, we immediately tend to imagine the other person becoming defensive or angry. The aim of this exercise is to flip this around so that you start to imagine the individual openly entering into a conversation about how they can improve, asking for your support as they do so.

- Once you have a list of positive outcomes, ask yourself "Who do I have to be during this interaction for this outcome to be true?" Asking this will allow you to plan how you will enter a situation with a mindset that is focused on delivering a positive outcome. Remember, you cannot control the outcome but you can determine who you are;

- Now close your eyes, take five deep breaths, and start to imagine how you will feel if the best happens. Feel your stress levels about the situation decrease as you experience a different and positive outcome;

- Relax, you've got this!

Roll with the Punches

As Tyson said, everyone has a plan until they get punched in the face. Being vulnerable, whilst not necessarily opening you up to physical punches, will open you up to emotional ones. And there is nothing you can do about it, apart from having a plan and the tools to help you deal with any issues.

Being fully vulnerable and leading with love will not be liked by everyone. This is a sad fact of life, and one, that if you are not willing to accept, then you are not willing to be the best person and leader that you can be. That may seem harsh, but if you cannot deal with the criticism of others, then you are still trying to please people around you.

I still feel nervous when I am about to be open and vulnerable in a new situation, and for me, that is a sign that I have not adopted another role, but I am being true to myself.

I plan. I make sure I have time after any new situation to allow myself to process the outcome, either to tap away any negative responses or hurt, or more often than not, to enjoy the open and loving occasion that occurred. I am still heartened and joyed by how most people respond. But I don't delude myself. I know for every person who responds warmly, there will be another who will judge harshly or simply ignore you.

It is critical that I am OK with that.

Exercise - How to survive a punch to the emotional face

Building your plan to deal with any emotional pain as quickly as you can means you can move on positively from situations that did not go as you hoped.

As an introvert, I plan "me" time every day, to ensure that I have the space I need to process and release anything that I have experienced that day. Sometimes, this is just five minutes by myself before I go to bed, others it is an hour or two, or a long walk in nature to ground me back into myself. Either way, I have to schedule this time so that I don't lose my passion to be vulnerable.

This is the process that I do, each Sunday, to ensure that I have time to deal with anything that may come up in the week.

- With your calendar open, identify times that will require you to be more vulnerable than usual, or new situations and experiences;

- Is there time after each one to give yourself five to 10 minutes to sit and process the outcome? If yes, schedule that as a private event in your calendar. Not only does active scheduling act as a reminder for you as you build this habit, but it also gives you the space and time to do so;

- If no, then when is the earliest time that you can make space? Notice the excuses that arise as you are finding this time. Notice any fear that may be coming up for you if you need to ask someone to make time;

- Once you have scheduled a short period of time for each event, next schedule two 30-minute slots, one on Wednesday and one Friday or Saturday to act as times for you to learn from the experiences;

- During these slots, write down any new fears or beliefs that arose and why you think you reacted in the way you did. Write down any ways in which you have grown. Did you handle a situation better than you thought you would? Did you connect with someone in a way that was unique? Notice both the learnings and the triumphs;

- Now celebrate, treat yourself in some way - you have led another week from your heart, and you are awesome!

FINDING YOUR MOTIVATION

So, how do you start to bring love back into your day and your people's day at work? The first step is to help you and the people around you find their "why". Why is the reason we act; Why is the reason we get out of bed and give our best; Why is what sets us apart from everyone else. And with the right why, we can change the world.

My "why" was elusive for a long time. I knew what I enjoyed doing, but I had not found that burning passion that drove me to deliver with excellence until I was forty. I had never really known what I had wanted to be when I grew up, and so I had done a combination of what was expected of me and what I enjoyed doing. But finding my why changed everything I do.

I have written about this previously, but my realisation that I wanted to change somehow and lead the world to be a better and different place was a nagging dream, and daydream. This vision would occur in my meditations and even on the train into work. I could visualise this scene over and over again, but I never knew what led to it or what I was actually doing in it. All I knew was that in this vision, at that very moment, I was precisely where I was meant to be, doing exactly what I was put on this earth to do.

In reality, the desire had been there since I was 17, when I first wanted to start writing about how I viewed the world, but fear and lack of confidence meant it took me much longer to find my voice.

So I had an outcome in mind, but never the motivation, drive, courage or notion for getting there. Hence why I think I spent so much of my life to date in relative inaction, I did not know why I should act.

Over a period of years, I started asking myself: What did this vision mean? Why was I there, on stage, in front of such bright lights and such a large crowd? What was I doing and why? To be honest, I was also slightly curious as to why I was always wearing yellow trousers in this vision, but in reality, that is most probably irrelevant.

For a long time, I got no answer in my meditation, and then I started to get the same phrase repeated over and over again, and it meant nothing to me because it seemed so blindingly obvious. I am here to love. That is all I kept on hearing and feeling; I am here to love. Well, duh, I thought, isn't everyone?

I ignored this, even though the phrase appeared, again and again. I even once saw it on an internet meme just after a meditation, but still, I pushed it to one side as it seemed so trite.

When I started my own business, I began pondering what would set me apart from all the other consultants in my field. I decided it was not going to be what I said or what services I offered, but rather how I made my customers feel. I decided that I was going to focus on my customer's emotions and embrace their problems with passion and compassion, so that they would end up feeling that I was the only consultant worth working with. I remember saying to a friend that "I am going to make my customers feel that I will love and support them through any issue they may be facing."

I still did not make the connection between what I had just said and the phrase I had repeatedly been hearing in my meditation. That penny only dropped about three months later!

I was chatting to an ex-colleague, and she was asking me if I was enjoying what I was doing. I was, and the reason was, I told her, was because I adored the people I was working with. I loved every single one of them; their uniqueness, their desire to be better for their customers, their belief that they could succeed. I remember saying that I was in love with every person I had seen that week. She looked at me as if I was mad, but also, knowing me as she does, not actually that surprised. It was her next comment that made me connect the dots.

"The way you love people brings you alive; you glow with such intensity." The way I love people, the way it made me feel to love people, brought me to life. It drove me to excel, it inspired me to go the extra mile, and it made me love others even more fiercely. It was then that I became conscious of what my purpose meant: I am here to love. I am here to come alive and glow by loving others. "I am here to love" is why I get out of bed in the morning. "I am here to love."

I worried for quite some time, that my desire to love the people around me was a mask for pleasing them, so I was scared to fall back into that trap. But as my understanding grew, I realised that I wanted to love others so that they could see their magnificence, their potential and everything they could be. As I peeled back the layers of my fear, I found anger. But a wave of righteous anger, at a world that hated excellence, that favoured and accepted mediocrity, that wanted everyone to stay small and insignificant. I wanted, longed, to give people the opportunity to truly see themselves for everything they could be, rather than play it safe and conform.

I have worked a number of roles since finding my why, and whilst I may have different titles and functions, my role has never changed. I am here to love. I am here to love my teams, my colleagues, my leaders, my customers and partners. I am not here just to do a job. Whilst I do do that job, I don't do it for that reason. I do it to make the lives of those around me easier. I do it so that people have space to grow and create in a nurturing environment. I do it so that I can love, and learn to love, everyone I come in contact with. The more I can learn to love, the stronger that love can be and the closer I can connect with others to show them what they are capable of.

I have found that by living my "why" has made people ask me for help in finding theirs, and that makes broaching the conversation more natural, especially when you start leading people down the path of living from your heart. So, find your why first, and then lead by example to help others find theirs.

I recently reheard the adage, "there is no competition for your life purpose". I used to think this was rather trite, but on reflection, I realised that what is means is that we are all unique, and, therefore, the value we can give is unique. There is, and will only ever be, one of each of us, so why do we lack the courage to leap and find what we are meant to give to this world?

This chapter is about finding your why at work, but you can easily translate this into any area of your life: your family, your hobby, or your health. Finding your why will give you the discipline to keep going when you want to give up, it will make those stressful times more enjoyable and it will provide you with an anchor to come back to when you need it. It will make you realise that, once and for all, not being mediocre is worth fighting for!

What is your "Why?"

Lots of people talk about finding their purpose but, for me, that was too abstract. I could come up with some grandiose statement that would make me feel smug, and as though I was going to make a difference, but it never made me act differently. For me, the paradigm shift of finding my "why" was because it changed the way I acted overnight. Action is what makes the difference, not just the intention or the dream. "Why" makes you go that one step further, gives you the courage to do what you fear, and allows you to lead and live through your heart in a way that nothing else can.

Like my entire journey, finding my why was an investigation. It entailed me digging deeper and questioning everything - every action, every thought, every relationship - what was the lesson I was trying to learn and why did it matter to me? It required me learning to listen to myself, others and the universe, and to learn to trust in the answer, even if I didn't know what it meant.

Doing this work on myself for my personal fulfilment takes time and commitment, but bizarrely, doing this for my professional life felt more comfortable. I think it is because we are accustomed to questioning our why at work. We appraise ourselves and our teams on a regular basis, and there is time and space for development conversations, so examining your why becomes more acceptable in a way. We also know that we are empowered, to a degree, to have conversations about engagement and happiness in the work place, which are not so easy to have at home.

But it is also tricky to detach the two. Our motivation is a driving force in everything we do, so surely the activities that motivate me at work should be similar to those at home. I also know that finding motivation is much easier when the sun is shining, compared with a rainy Tuesday morning, so creating a process that was going to be replicable for others was going to be tricky.

What I found was that my motivation was a mixture of knowing what I wanted to achieve, in a sense, knowing my destination, combined with why I felt it was so important to go there. I could not intellectualise my motivation; it is a feeling that drives me. It is a force rather than a thought process. The power of knowing where I want to get to and why, is what makes me aware when I am procrastinating. It gives me the strength to sit at my desk and write, or head to the pool when I need to. It gives me the courage to be willing to be different, and it keeps my faith alive when life is tough.

My why is the feeling I get when I look into someone's eyes when they have succeeded when they thought they would fail. My why is the joy I feel when my team truly celebrates what it can do together, and my why is the infectious enthusiasm of a member of staff with a new idea. My why is the spark of potential, which we so often extinguish in ourselves, when it comes alive and takes root. My why is creating an environment where others can thrive and believe in themselves. My why is creating a space where people feel safe to believe that dreams can happen and so they try.

Getting to the root of your why requires peeling back the layers. All of us immediately tend to create logical and head-lead reasons; my immediate reason was that I wanted to be successful and enjoy what I did. But that is not a why that is going to motivate you during the tough times. It is a reason that all of us will have and it is not unique to drive you to deliver the value that only you can give to the world.

For a while, I was happy with these answers, but I quickly noticed that they did not give me the get-up and go that I was looking for. I decided that I was going to dedicate a week of nightly meditations and journaling to find the root of my why; the driving force that would get me out of bed on the dark, cold days.

The first night, I sat down and I wrote down my purpose of wanting to change the world by loving more and then my primary reasons why. After each reason, I stopped and asked myself "what is the reason behind this why?" For example, why do I want to be successful? Because I want to build a quality of life that lets me lead a life of travel and adventure. Building on this reason, I then asked, why do I want to lead a life of travel and adventure? Because I want to see more, meet more people, and learn more about all of the different places and cultures on this planet.

I did this over and over again, sometimes going in a different direction, but each night I got to the same root reason. I want to help more people reach their highest potential and be everything they can be.

I then started testing this why outside of my professional life. Did this resonate with my kids, my family, my friends? It was at this point that I knew I had found my why. It was this moment when I realised that this motivation permeated every area of my life; that this why was going to give me the drive to be better every single day, in everything I did. I knew what my purpose was, why I would be willing to stand out from the crowd and do what needed to be done to ensure I achieved it.

TEAM BUILDING FRAMEWORK

For years I have instinctively looked to build a culture that allows trust to thrive in my teams. When I started out, I wanted everyone to like each other, to get on, and I realised that it was irrelevant. What a team needs to know is that their leader and peers will have each other's backs in time of stress. And there are always times of stress in a corporate environment and in life, in general.

But this takes time, and needs to be created carefully, to ensure that everyone has an equal voice and that you all have the chance to contribute. Over a few years, I created a framework that sets the scene for trust to build. However, you cannot artificially create trust, it has to grow authentically, and, therefore, it requires you, as a leader, to trust first.

I mix and match each aspect, based on the age of the team, how long people have worked together and the seniority of the members. Do what feels right.

The framework I describe below has three aspects, which I have detailed in a way that will allow you to lead your teams through the process. In the resources section, I have also added more links and places to go to for further information. The three steps are:

- Know who you are and who your team are;

- Be aware of how you react;

- Understand your life priorities and those of your team.

Know Who You and Your Team Are

Trust needs people to be vulnerable, be able to understand each other's context and give each other the space to communicate in a way that feels right for each individual. It is not about knowing the life history of every member of your team, or their deepest hopes and fears, but it is about understanding their context.

Context is everything in creating a space for people to understand each other. People from different cultural and family set-ups all have different backgrounds, and this impacts how we all respond to situations.

When I first started managing teams from across the world, I was given a lot of cultural awareness training. Whilst in itself there is a lot of value that can be garnered from such sessions, I found the cultural stereotyping and classification of some cultures less helpful than the skill to question others about their context. We all have several cultural norms that we have adopted growing up, but in my experience, that is just the tip of the iceberg when it comes to understanding individuals and their behaviours.

Having spent much of my career in sales, knowing how my customer's buying process may differ from culture to culture is critical, especially when planning lead times, etc., but I found it would not predict how effective my methods were. I needed to tailor myself to each customer, not each culture. The same was true for leading global teams. Yes, certain techniques would work better, as a rule, in some cultures over others, but to truly get the best out of my teams, I needed to know their individual context.

Different personality types will also react differently in similar environments. Having an awareness of these factors gives a team a starting point to understand each other and listen to different viewpoints.

There are numerous tools to help you to start to define your teams personality types and I am sure you can think of hundreds of questions that would allow a team member to share their personal context in a non-invasive way, but below are the tools that I have used successfully over the years. Feel free to tailor the recommendations below to suit your needs and beliefs.

To allow me and my team to understand their personality traits, I use the 16personalities.com test available on their website. This questionnaire is a Jungian-based tool, which incorporates Myers Briggs, as well as much more of their own research, and they have made it more relatable by creating a character name for each personality type.

The critical aspect to note is that this is not just about you, the team leader, understanding your team's personality types. They need to know their own and those around them, to allow them to move towards being a high functioning team.

It is also by combining personality typing with a personal context that you can understand how you and your team members will react to certain situations.

I ask my team to take the test, but I make it optional for them to share the results and I encourage them to share as I strongly believe this helps teams grow stronger, but if anyone wanted to keep their information confidential, I would wholeheartedly support that. Interestingly, I have never had anyone refuse to tell the rest of the team what type they are.

I generally ask teams to do this before getting together for a day. I want them to have time to read and digest their results prior to sharing. I ask them to spend some time reflecting on the result, and I ask them to answer the following questions, which again, they don't have to share the answers to, but mostly they do:

- Does this personality type feel right to you?

- If one of your close friends or family members read this personality would they recognise you in it?

- Pick two weaknesses and think about how you display these in times of stress, at home or work. How do you behave?

- Pick two strengths and think about how you display these in your life. Could these behaviours be useful to the wider team?

- Can you link any of these behaviours to previous experiences in your life?

- If yes, what were these experiences and how do you think they continue to impact your behaviour?

This self-reflection, as part of the process, is so crucial in my view, as it is the first step of people becoming aware of who they are. Often, I have found that there are some people in a team who embrace this wholeheartedly having done something similar previously, or they just have a natural interest in themselves and their personal development.

But for others, this will be brand new in the workplace. The concept that who you are and the experiences you have had can impact your ability to be a team player is not new, but we are only just starting to look at how we incorporate this into our everyday professional lives. I have always used this point as a moment to check-in with each team member individually, to see how they are reacting and to gauge their level of enthusiasm for engaging in such discussions. This check-in gives me the insight to know what I need to do when I bring the team together.

Team meetings are day to day events for many of us, but it is only usually once a quarter or every six months that most teams come together to develop as a team, rather than work on the day to day stuff. I think we underestimate this time together, and we do so at the detriment of the team. You should be able to include conversations like this on a weekly or monthly basis, either formally or informally, but that takes time, understanding and willingness.

When a team meets together as a group for the first time, I start to talk about the strengths and weaknesses of each personality, making it clear that these strengths and weaknesses are not fixed, but a trait that a particular personality type may exhibit under certain situations. I also talk through the difference between introvert and extrovert.

Most people are quite surprised when they discover that I am an introvert; I have to admit, I was when I first found out myself. But once I was aware of what that meant, I started to study my behaviour. I examined how I seemed to push people away when I was stressed or tired and just wanted to hide in my room. As I started to understand my personality traits and then I layered the context of having grown up in a boarding school, where you never get time to yourself, I began to understand why my tendency to push people away was so extreme. Extreme to the point where I could cut people off when stressed or fly off the handle and demand to be left alone if someone innocently asked me if I was OK.

Knowing your traits is one thing, but understanding how they exhibit themselves in your life allows you to communicate with people ahead of time. I now always tell my team that I am an introvert and that in times of "stress", I will need to carve out time to step away, regroup and meditate. It allows the people around me to understand how they can support me to be better and more effective, and as I start to talk them through my strengths and weaknesses, I often get people volunteering theirs and how they tend to react.

It is important to stress that weaknesses are not bad things as such. We all have off days, you may be ill, or the kids had a bad night, or you are suffering from jet lag. Any of these stressors will make you more likely to display one or more of your personality traits' weaknesses. It does not mean that you are weak. Quite the opposite. I am often amazed at the commitment and resilience of people who continue to show up and perform under significant stress. But we all know that when we are having one of these days, we are more likely to snap or can disengage more easily.

And that is why, as simplistic as it may seem, these conversations are the starting point of building a mutual awareness of each other, and often lead to much more profound and more productive conversations about what each team member needs from those around the table.

The other lightbulb moment that always occurs when we start talking about strengths, is that at some point someone will say something like, "I wish I could do that" or "I wish I were more like you sometimes". This is the moment where you can start to help the team understand that they are stronger and better together. If you are aware that you are not good at public speaking, for example, but for a peer it comes naturally, using their support to help you through the preparation for your next presentation starts building the connections across the team to support each other. This level of team understanding allows individuals to see who can "augment" them in times of stress or support.

The key is for everyone to start seeing and understanding how they can be better together, rather than as individuals.

One observation I have often made is that it is frequently those who don't naturally gravitate towards each other, who can offer the most support. Having open conversations around our strengths and weaknesses, in a safe environment, breaks down the possibility of cliques forming within a team, as this process is not about friendship. It becomes about being better in your role. The more connections that are made across a team, the stronger it is, and the more likely it is to grow, succeed and excel through tough times.

These connections also allow for personal relationships to form, and the moment this happens, people start to care about each other. They start seeing the value and worth in each member of the team, then love and trust can beginning to develop. This process is not about liking everyone, but this is about caring for each other in a way that creates a safe environment for people to grow, learn, fail and develop together.

Individual context is critical to understanding how personality traits are displayed by each person, so give time for reflection and discussion. Having spent some time understanding each other's personality traits, I then move on to helping them understand their context.

I rarely move on to this step on the same day as looking at a team's personality traits, but I would follow it up as day two on a retreat. But I have also successfully continued to grow an environment of trust and love with a six-month gap between each session, so do what feels right for you and your team.

Example 3 - How do I build trust and influence as a team leader if I have been internally promoted over my peers?

A promotion is not a reward, it is a new job, and you need to approach it in that way. Much like stepping in as a new leader from outside the company (see Example 2), you have to cope with legacy issues and relationships. This becomes significantly harder if you used to be a member of that team but the recipe for success is the same. Listen, Observe, Learn, Suggest.

Be mindful of your behaviours and change them, if necessary, to your new job. Whilst you are the same person, and may wish to be treated as such, you have a different job, with different stakeholders and objectives. You will need to shift your perspective.

Context is an odd thing, it does not give you answers as such, but it gives you pointers. I am not a trained psychologist, but years of observing people and how they react within a team has given me some insight into what I will expect from people. They are not always accurate, but a rule of thumb.

Those born into larger families tend to feel more comfortable in groups or group activities. However, I have observed that they are also less likely to speak up as larger family groups, whilst loud and noisy, are not always conducive to active listening. I know I need to spend time ensuring that these individuals feel heard and listened to.

Those people who moved regularly as children don't necessarily adapt to change better or faster, but they are more accepting that change is an on-going part of life. So, I need to make sure that I support them as much through any change, but I may not have to spend as much time explaining the reason for the change.

Bizarrely, in my experience, those born in cities are more open to sharing their opinions compared with people who grew up in villages. I have found those who grew up in village environments are more used to people knowing their stories, but crave privacy more than city kids. Again, these are generalisations that I have observed, not hard and fast rules.

Knowledge and observations, like these, have allowed me to become a more effective leader, as I can tailor how I spend my energy on each team member, to ensure that they feel supported and valued.

Questions to help share individual context:

- How many siblings do you have?

- Where did you grow up? City, town or village

- Did you play team sports as a child? At what level?

- How many houses did you live in before your 18th birthday?

- Did you enjoy school?

- What was your favourite subject at school?

- Do you have children?

Each question gives more insight, and I have yet to find someone who is not comfortable sharing this level of detail about their life with their colleagues. Often these questions prompt more sharing, if that happens, let it. The more we know about each other, the better.

I share these questions ahead of time and then ask the teams to split into pairs or groups of three to share their answers. The key is that this fits in with personality types. For example, I am an introvert, from a big family, that moved a lot. For me, peace and quiet are heavenly. I crave it, especially when I am stressed, I need time to process my feelings and what is happening around me, but I am also welcoming of change and enjoy it. As a team member, this means that whilst I often need space, I am not used to asking for it, as it was not really an option growing up, so I ask those around me to push me to take time out if they think I need it.

With such an insight, those around me know how to engage with me better when I am stressed, they know what I need to get back to high performance, and they support me better. The combination of context and personality type gives an emotion-free framework to offer active and relevant support when it is needed the most.

Once each team member has the chance to share within the smaller groups, I then pull the whole team together again to talk about what they learnt about each other. This part of the process for me is very organic. Each team is unique, so let them be just that.

So, the first step to building a culture that allows trust and love to thrive is to give people a greater awareness of themselves and each other in a way that removes emotion. But, it is critical to note that you cannot do this from day one as a new team leader. Your team needs to have a fundamental element of trust in you as a human being before you can start to create this safe environment. Don't rush or push through this process. Trust your intuition to know when the team is ready. This does not mean each member of the team has to trust you fully in order for you to start, but you need to have the momentum of trust in you, a leader, from the majority of your team, to take everyone on the journey. Again, note that this does not mean your team have to like you, they just need to know that they can trust you.

Conversations like these usually take a number of days, with regular breaks, and time to reflect. I often ask my teams to break every hour and spend five to 10 minutes alone or in a small group, reflecting on what they have learnt about themselves. Always trade speed for depth of reflection and sharing. This patience will pay you dividends in the long run and trying to speed up this process will make it lose its authenticity.

What of the things you have learnt excite you, scare you, or you simply don't want to believe?

No matter how confident or self-assured someone is, there will be aspects of themselves that they may not like - this can be tough to digest and it always takes time. Allow people to think about what they are learning and give them space as individuals, as well as a team, to figure out how they want to take this knowledge further.

Be Aware of How You React

We all have bad days, it is part of life that makes it exciting, and this means we react differently from one day to the next. Whilst this makes life fun, it also means that how you interact and are experienced by others will change depending on how you react.

I first became aware of this following a 1:1 with one of my team members. She confessed to me that she was never sure which Helen was going to show up in times of stress. This confession shook me for a couple of reasons. Firstly, she was a friend of mine, as well as a team member, so I thought she knew me, and secondly, I wanted to be the type of leader who was consistent and reliable for my team, but how could I be, if someone I thought I was close to experienced me as erratic?

I decided to take some time to observe how I reacted, and I started to notice that stress and change had an interesting impact on me. I like change, and I adapt to it quickly, but I still go through all the normal change stages that everyone else does. However, I realised that because I went through the steps so quickly, I seemed to go through them very intensely. If I was scared or angry about something that was going on around me, I was very scared or very angry. I adapted quickly, but I adapted deeply. Those around me who worked through change at a slower pace, seemed to exhibit the stages more subtly. I experienced extremes of emotions that only lasted for about 72 hours, but could throw those around me significantly.

Those who understood me knew to step back and give me space to process, but those who did not, found it unnerving and difficult to deal with. I decided that I had to become more and more aware of how I was reacting in the here and now. I researched teachings and techniques to give me the vocabulary to start to understand how I reacted and interacted, and I found the most effective and applicable in the workplace was a combination of Transactional Analysis and the Mindset work by Carol Dweck.

For those of you new to Transactional Analysis, this methodology was built by Eric Berne in the 1950s, as he started to dive into the multi-faceted nature of human beings in his practice as a psychotherapist. His observed that people "played' in three primary states: Adult, Child and Parent; during any social interaction. His work gave me a framework to understand and analyse my behaviours in a way that I could do something with, and it also gave me a language to express myself in.

I am not an expert in Transactional Analysis, and I urge you to read more, especially Berne's brilliant book "Games People Play", first published in 1964, but I have used it for many years to give people the vocabulary to express themselves and their responses, in a way that others can relate to.

Below, I have, in my own words, given my layperson's view of the three primary states. For a more comprehensive definition please go to www.ericberne.com

- Adult - the state where you feel in control and able to converse freely, honestly and without being led by your emotional response. This response does not mean that you are emotionless, but you are responsible for your emotions and understand how they are making you react. You are in a state where you are analysing the data that you are receiving and responding in a rational and appropriately measured way;

- Parent - this state is given to us, in a way, and embedded in our programming from an early age, by how we see others; usually, how those older than us, react and respond to situations. It is an automatic response that we have picked up from our external environment and culture. This state has two sub-states that have emerged, and I find them useful in classifying how I am reacting, but they are not the pure state as defined by Berne. In very simplistic terms, the parent state means we react how we have been taught to;

- Nurturing Parent - you want to help do things for others. In the workplace, this would often exhibit itself as someone taking on more work, rather than allowing others to do it and learn for themselves, or being concerned about giving honest feedback as it may hurt another's feelings. This reaction doesn't want to rock the boat or cause confrontation;

- Critical Parent - nothing is ever good enough. Professionally, this is often experienced by others as someone whose standards are close to perfection and cannot abide mistakes; they are difficult to please and quick to give harsh feedback without taking the time to teach and coach others;

- Child - I view this state as the one where emotion leads. A child response happens when we react emotionally based on a previous emotional response. These emotional responses we have learnt as young children from how we have emotionally interpreted and event. There are also two sub-states to Child.

- Adaptive Child - quick to please and avoid confrontation at all cost. At work, this is likely to be seen in an individual just saying yes without questioning why. When I react from this state, I know I am hiding from something, either a tough conversation or dealing with a historic issue. I sometimes use this state to give me time and space to think. I will agree to something in a meeting, or not voice my opinion, as I don't feel I have all the facts or analysis to do otherwise. It is not an adult response, which would be "I need more time or data to give you an answer". But in times of stress, I have found it gave me breathing space without having to be vulnerable;

- Rebellious or Natural Child - this is the curious part of us. The three-year-old who is always asking why, or the inner teenager who refuses to agree and wants to push boundaries. In a way, I love this state, as it can change conversations or drive innovation. But misunderstood, and you are stuck in a loggerhead situation with a belligerent teenager. Being able to catch your emotional reaction as a Rebellious Child and use that curiosity in the Adult state can be incredibly creative but requires discipline.

During any one day, we can move between all three of these states, and sub-states, on numerous occasions, and different people will make us more likely to fall into one reaction than others. There are various reasons why we may respond in one way over another, and no reaction is bad, as such, but the more we can be in an Adult state, the more constructive and supportive we can be as a leader and colleague.

None of these states are bad. At different points in our lives and during different experiences we have used each one to help us. There is a theory that the rebellious teenage child was the reason we left the Rift Valley and migrated as a race, but if you understand how you are reacting, you can choose to change to a more productive state if necessary.

Another aspect of Transactional Analysis that I like is that if you are reacting in one state, it is quite often the case that whomever you are interacting with, is reacting in a related state or will quickly move into that state. What I mean by this is, if you are being a Nurturing Parent, whomever you are with will often be in a Child state, either Rebellious or Adaptive depending on their context. If you are reacting from a Child state, the other party will often be Parent. This knowledge means that the more you can react from an Adult state, the more likely it is that others will react the same way.

For me, this awareness is not about removing my emotions from my interactions. In fact, I believe we need to bring more emotion into our professional lives, but we need to do it constructively and mindfully. It is not about quashing emotions but about giving people an understanding of what is driving their emotions. It is OK to be angry about a decision made at work, as long as that anger is due to the decision made at work, not in response to a similar situation that happened 30 years ago.

I used to hate getting feedback. My grandparents were happy to critique, and often did so in a manner that was meant to keep you down or in your place. Feedback, for me, always made me feel as though I was about to endure a personal attack and that I was never going to live up to someone's expectations. In most of my appraisals or 1:1s early in my career, I would swing between

Adaptive Child, agree to everything just to get the experience over and done with, or Rebellious Child, "screw you and what you think, you're wrong". I never saw these as opportunities to learn and get better. I was very much in a Fixed Mindset when it came to how I reacted to feedback and acted from a child state consequentially.

In Carol Dweck's brilliant book, Mindset, she states that there are two primary mindsets that people fall into: growth and fixed. A fixed mindset is just that - unable to learn and adapt to the best of its ability and, in my opinion, tends to be there to protect the ego's view of self. It is the A grade student, devastated and mortified by getting a B, instead of figuring out what they need to learn more about. A growth mindset, on the other hand, sees everything as an opportunity to learn and improve. It is the part of us that is willing to put in the effort to get better at a task or to figure out what went wrong.

Like our ego states in Transactional Analysis, you can swing between a fixed and a growth mindset, numerous times per day. I find that I tend to be more open to being in a growth mindset at work than I do when doing something physical. I lack patience with myself when I am trying to learn how to get better at something like skiing or swimming, but I am willing to put the effort in at work. Each of us will have areas in our lives where it feels more natural to be in a growth mindset and be more curious. But having an awareness of which mindset you are in allows you to, again, make a deliberate choice about how you will respond to any given situation.

Over time, and with practice, we can get better and faster at recognising where we, and those around us, are reacting from and change accordingly. We don't need to improve ourselves and our characters, but having the knowledge and the ability to adapt our response to our environment means that we can connect and communicate with others more effectively. That is critical to building a thriving, high performing, team environment.

I introduce these frameworks to all of the teams I lead and am given the chance to work with, as the ability to have a vocabulary to articulate your reaction in any given point in time is invaluable. But these frameworks are complicated, and I urge people to read the original work before diving in.

Whilst these frameworks have allowed me to know more about myself, and those around me, I have still had to do a significant amount of work to "deal" with the reactions I have been programmed with, or have learnt growing up. Knowing how you will or won't react is one thing, but encourage your teams to also look at how to change how they respond, if they wish to grow.

Choosing Your Priorities

As we move through life, our priorities change. At one time, we are willing to dedicate more energy to our careers, at other times it is our home lives that will take most of our focus. But for some reason, in most workplaces, we expect our staff to give the same amount of energy and priority to their jobs every day of the year and each year of their working life. This is unrealistic.

Now, I am not condoning poor or low performance, but we have to acknowledge, as leaders and members of a team, that not everyone will be able, or willing, to give everything to their roles all of the time. This fact does not mean that they won't do excellent work, but it may mean that they are not willing to travel on a Sunday or work every evening, and that needs to be respected. But it can only be respected, and boundaries understood, if we are transparent enough with each other that we know where our focus is.

Earlier this year, I was training for an Ironman 70.3. It was getting closer to the race and, several times a week, I needed to be on a bike for three or more hours at a time. Whilst I did this out of traditional work hours, this did mean that I was not "online" as much as my team had become used to. Anticipating this, I shared this with them and told them when I would not be around, so that they could give me the chance to give my best to my training and also to them. It gave me space to dedicate energy to my team and to my training in an appropriate way. For a few weeks of this year, I made a conscious and transparent choice to prioritise my training over my inbox.

I have done the same during busy sales times, or when specific projects need my time and attention. If we don't set our priorities transparently about where and how we are going to put our attention, then the expectation will be that we place an equal amount of energy and attention into everything we do. And that's where madness and burn out lives!

We may be able to have it all, but we can't do it all, in the same way, at the same time. Time is incredibly precious, it is the only thing we cannot get back, so we need to use it wisely and with purpose.

There is a simple exercise that I do with myself, and teams, every quarter. I ask them to draw the pie chart below, changing the size of the sections to show where their focus has been in the last three months, where it is now and what they want it to be in the three months going forward.

It is rare that anyone has equal sections. At some point, each of us sacrifices something in our lives for other parts of it. The difference is whether we are choosing to do this deliberately or whether it is thrust upon us. For example, I have two small children. Therefore, I have, for the last few years, sacrificed my time with friends and my vocation (or hobby), to spend more time with my family. I know this is not sustainable and something that I am rebalancing, but making that conscious choice meant that I could a) tell my friends and b) fit in time with my family alongside a hectic work schedule.

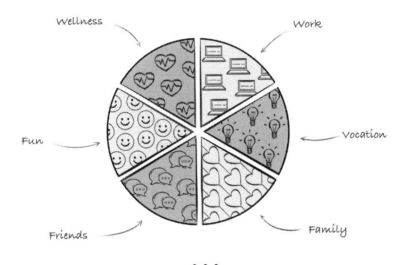

. . .

I ask my teams to draw and share their priorities. Not to call out poor performers or people who are looking to coast (they are addressed individually), but to allow people the opportunity to share what is going to be important to them in the next few months that they may need support on.

For example, if a team member is planning their wedding, they may not have as much focus on other parts of their lives, or may need more support given to them from other members of the team in the run-up to the big day and covering their honeymoon. These requests are not about picking up the slack for another but giving each other the awareness to know how to operate better as a team. When I was training for my Ironman 70.3, we still exceeded our sales target, and my team felt fully supported, but they knew that on a Friday evening, come 5 pm, I was on a bike for three hours, and if they called, they would get a conversation filled with heavy breathing or I simply would not pick up the phone.

Combining all of these tools does not create a high performing team overnight, but it does start to form the culture and behaviours where love, trust and, thus, high performance can thrive. Having a culture that unites a team in love, trust and integrity, allows you to start having conversations that lead to better performance.

Unity in direction, strategy and action is the secret to high-performance, and this can only be accomplished in a team that loves, trust and believes in themselves and each other.

COLLABORATION, CREATIVITY AND CONFLICT

I have worked in a number of industries and companies of all sizes in my career, and the common denominator in all of them is that they are all wanting more creativity and collaboration from their staff; they want teams who innovate.

I have seen various processes and technologies applied to help drive collaborative behaviours and innovation, but I have concluded that none of this will work unless there is a safe and loving culture that encourages conflict and debate.

It may seem like an oxymoron to suggest that love and conflict go hand in hand, but they are intrinsically linked if you want to drive a culture of collaboration and creativity. People have to feel safe to disagree without repercussions, as long as it is done from a place of love and respect. Being open to debate a concept or problem allows for different perspectives and ideas to be heard and built upon. A culture which is hierarchical or errs on the side of passive aggressive will never lead to fresh thinking.

My theory on this is simple. Conflict creates friction, and when done in the right way, in a loving environment, friction can lead to a stronger understanding of each other and sparks creativity.

Collaboration is about working effectively together, not just together, to meet a shared outcome. But it also requires a deep understanding of the people who you are working with to be sustainable and authentic. Otherwise, you end up with a culture where everyone is included in everything, and it all starts to feel like six-year-olds playing football. Everyone is chasing the ball, and you lose sight of the bigger picture and direction. Collaboration, managed appropriately, can transform a business, but more often than not, it causes decision paralysis and too many meetings.

If each player on a team knows their role, they can know when to pull in the right people, aligning this with a culture that allows space and time for all voices to be heard appropriately and can ensure collaboration is carried out when needed, not just for the sake of being seen as a "team player".

The on-going craze to move to a matrix structure has allowed collaboration to get out of control and quash creativity. We are now too busy making sure that everyone knows everything, rather than using collaboration as the tool it is, to allow ideas and opinions to be voiced, heard, discussed, argued over, refined and perfected.

Good collaboration can lead to conflicting opinions, not the passive-aggressive nodding of heads that is all too common in most meeting rooms today. I don't think people actively shy away from a safe conflict conversation, but I think many have too little time to genuinely form and voice a relevant opinion, as we are just too busy sharing data.

In a crisis, people come together and forge fantastic teams, but these quickly fall to the wayside when you remove the pressure, because the environment was not authentic or based on a foundation of trust and a mutual understanding of how each party can add value. The key lies in creating a culture of curiosity in each other and the different perspectives we all bring. Hence, I always recommend starting with the team building framework before leaping into collaborative creativity. This culture building requires work and patience as a leader.

Love leadership requires that you can make, and hold, space and time for your people to get to understand each other and their context, whilst simultaneously delivering what your business needs. This effort is not for the faint hearted, or those that just want to dictate, and line manage. It requires not demanding that your team "get to know each other", but rather that they spend the time listening and engaging with each other, viewing the world, role, or problem from someone else's shoes.

Spending time getting to know the names of your team's children or pets is fine and important, but it will not deliver long term success. What will deliver, is spending time understanding who they are, how they will react in certain circumstances, and how you can make them become the best they can be. Allow each of them to do the same for their peers. Then give the time, space and respect to disagree and bounce ideas around. Give them a chance to create and play with your biggest business problems, instead of forcing them into endless meetings.

Your people need to feel safe expressing ideas or opinions that may be considered as "out there", and they have to feel safe enough to make mistakes and be wrong. Even harder, they need to be willing to listen to different opinions around the room. If each team member knows the value and strengths they bring to the team, they are less willing to be defensive when confronted with the fact that they may not have the solution for the problem at hand. Admitting you don't know the answer, or you have made a mistake, is hard, and no one ever feels 100% comfortable doing it. But we need to be willing to learn and develop our thinking, i.e. to innovate.

I have learnt that, as a leader, I should be giving my opinion and views last, so that I can dedicate my energy to listening to the thoughts from others first. This also removes any temptation for people to "please the boss" by agreeing with you, as they don't know where you stand.

Make collaboration and conflict inviting, and the process fun, and you can only get creativity, innovation and a better performing team as the outcome.

LET'S CELEBRATE

One strength I have noticed over and over again in teams that genuinely love and care for each other, is that they celebrate. They celebrate the significant milestones, the small wins and each other, with a passion. They are proud of what they achieve together, and they want to share their joy with the world. It is infectious and engaging.

Having spent most of my career in sales, hitting milestones is a given if you want to be successful, but true celebration is not. I initially thought that a culture of competitiveness and celebration could not happen together, but in a strong love culture, they live side by side and actually enhance each other.

Praise in raising children is vital; it allows us to demonstrate to the child our pride in their effort, not solely the outcome. The same is true in leadership. Celebration can be about the outcome, but it gains power and momentum when it is about the effort.

Praising and celebrating effort creates a culture where trying something new is welcomed. Praising and celebrating effort turns failure into learning opportunities and curiosity. As a leader and a manager, we expect our teams to work hard, but we have started only to reward the outcome. Turning up to work every day and giving your all is not easy, and yet in our current corporate culture, it has become an expectation. I feel that this is a pity as just the intention of showing up and giving your all should be lauded not expected.

But we need to be careful that we don't use praise and celebration to hide from the tough conversations that need to be had for a team to succeed. But there needs to be equal proportions of praise and improvement for continuous growth and learning to happen.

But maybe more powerfully the act of celebration, the act of stopping for even just five minutes to praise the effort that has happened, pulls us back into the moment, and into the unity that forms a team.

We move so quickly from task to task, to rush through the to-do list that we rarely stop and reflect on what has just happened. If we do, it is likely that we then shine a spotlight on it and ask others to celebrate with us.

Example 4 - Enforced Socialisation

There is the old adage that teams are forged at the bar. I disagree with this. Friendships are formed at the bar, and whilst I have made some great friends at work, this does not make a high-performing team. A team needs to understand their objectives, and the job that each person does within the team, to achieve them. This does not require spending time at a bar or any other social team building. I am not trying to be a killjoy, I am often the first to buy a round, but it is important to distinguish between building teams and having social fun at work with colleagues.

The more you do understand each other and personal context, the more effective a team can be. There needs to be time for teams to get to share their traits and contexts in a work environment. Heading to the bar to celebrate is one thing, but make sure people don't feel it's compulsory. Also, limit the work talk in social environments. Team members need to choose their priorities to match what they want to achieve in their lives, and that could be their family, their hobby, or their health, over and above spending time with colleagues outside of work hours. As a leader, you need to support and encourage this. No member of your team should feel at a disadvantage because they did not go out for dinner or a drink.

Celebration pulls people together. It gives us a chance to stop and be grateful for what we can do individually, or together, as a team. So, next time you or your team have accomplished anything, an epic win or a mundane activity, take the time to celebrate it openly. Praise the effort that was put in, acknowledge the learning, the growth, and celebrate the outcome. I have also noticed that celebration is infectious; it makes people want to get involved; it drives engagement. In a day and age when more and more people are disengaged from their jobs, celebration plays a multi-pronged role.

It is easy to publicise our achievements, through social media or another marketing medium, but we tend to focus on the abilities of our products, rather than the actions of the teams who build and put those products and services in the hands of the consumer. I find this sad, as we are praising the wrong thing. Our products and services would never exist without the people around them who innovate, nurture and deliver them.

The simplicity of stopping with your team for a coffee together is enough to allow you to come and recognise what you can achieve as one.

Celebrate loud, celebrate proudly and feel the energy and vigour it will bring to your team. Praise the effort, not the outcome, and watch the bonds strengthen between your people and your customers.

STAYING TRUE

It doesn't interest me if the story you are telling me is true.
I want to know if you can disappoint another to be true to yourself.
If you can bear the accusation of betrayal and not betray your own soul.
If you can be faithless and therefore trustworthy.

• • •

I love this verse from The Invitation. It reminds me that we need to take our dreams, our passions and our talents, seriously. We need to be willing to stand up and potentially betray those around us, to become everything we could be. We need to be fearless in our pursuit of giving value. But, I am also careful not to take myself too seriously; you need to have a sense of humour to live from your heart, so that you can laugh at yourself and what you still need to learn.

The universe and all the people in it need us to be the best we can, our nearest and dearest need the same. However, sometimes it can be easier to be true to a stranger, than the person in the same room, as over time we change and learn and, therefore, may need to disappoint another to be true to ourselves, and that is one of the scariest things I have faced.

If the soul has a seat in the body, it is in the heart, the core of our chest which pumps the lifeblood around our very beings. Living from your heart requires you to be consistent and as faithful as its beat and as critical to those you engage with as the oxygen carried in your red blood cells. Safety and sanctity are not commodities that are available to you when you truly love from your heart, you must be willing to risk it all for everyone and anyone, to put your truth out there for the world to see and judge, and yet, not be held back by the fear of rebuttal.

You must open, trust, and hear your heart sing in its loudest voice. Trust that what it says can lead to no harm and follow its tune. Sacrifice all for love, give up the pursuit of money, fame and luxury for that of compassionate and loving certainty. Know that your heart is leading you in all you do and that its wisdom knows no end. It is boundless, beyond limits and cannot be tamed, but it can be wielded to right wrongs and bring joy, gratitude and abundance to all.

In a moment of meditation, I wrote the following passage. I feel that it is fitting to be the end of this book, as it is my prayer for myself, and for anyone else who is willing to lead more with love, and attempt to bring about the paradigm shift this world and our corporate cultures need.

My Heart's Prayer

I will never lead you astray, but I will demand courage of you. I will demand that you learn and listen. And if you fail to do either, I will send you back to the beginning. Don't tame me; do not give me boundaries in which to act. If you let me free, I am free for good.

I can give you your heart's desire, for I have that power, but I will only give you that which you truly require. I will accept no substitutes, no half measures. In me there is ecstasy and freedom. I, alone, have the power to release you from all expectations. To let you soar and thrive. I only ask that you give me your all, your everything, and your trust.

Be true to me. Release the power you have inside you; you do not need to control it, it will not overpower you, but help you reach mastery. It will show you the way and give you the light you need to shine. Let my knowledge be your indicator of what is right and what is wrong. I know the difference, even before you know the question. Surrender to me, and I will let you shine brighter than you could ever imagine.

Surrender to me. Let it not be a choice of the mind, but one that every cell in your body screams the answer to in unison; yes! Let me give you a life of flow and ease. Surrender to the natural ebb and flow of the universe. I am prompting you to speak and act in a manner of loving defiance. You can never be off track if you let me lead.

I am your calling, I am your voice, and I am the star in your story, so let me shine. Let me take you to soar to such heights that you could not fathom the distance you have come, or the life of joy that you lead. Let me comfort you when you need rest and motivate you when you need drive. Let me love you completely. Let me love.

My Notes

My Notes

My Notes

My Notes

My Notes

My Notes

RESOURCES

Throughout this book, I have mentioned people or techniques that I have found useful or have inspired me to try something different, such as tapping. Below is a list of those books, websites and people who I have mentioned. Please check out their work, as they have such value to add:

- Mindset by Carol Dweck
- The Power of Now by Eckhart Tolle
- The Tapping Solution - www.thetappingsolution.com
- Brendon Burchard - www.brendon.com
- The Invitation by Oriah Mountain Dreamer
- You Can Heal Your Life - Louise Hay
- Love Yourself, Heal Your Life - Louise Hay
- Transactional Analysis - http://www.ericberne.com/transactional-analysis/
- Games People Play - Eric Berne

ACKNOWLEDGEMENTS

The process of writing a book is hard work and requires dedication, and that can mean you don't have as much time for those around you as before. I would like to take the time to thank my sons, for giving me the time and space to write.

I want to thank all those around who encouraged and supported me, who never doubted my ability to finish, even when I did, and who genuinely thought that this was not one of my craziest ideas.

I would also like to thank Stephanie Long, Isabel Ehrlich and Charlotte Wyld, for giving me their honest feedback about the book as it neared completion. Jane Thomas, Lily Silverton-Parker and Pat Chapman-Pincher were instrumental in turning something good, into something very readable, and easy to put into action.

I wrote this book to learn about myself, what sort of person I was, and how I could become the leader I want to be. Whilst the concept of publishing it was always there in my mind, it was never the driver for what I wrote. I wrote as a way to discover everything that was holding me back. It was a way to reflect on my life, the lessons I have learnt from, the experiences I keep repeating, and the aspects of myself that I would rather hide from and forget about. It has been a journey in many ways. The discipline of sitting down every day and putting words on paper has taught me that I can stick to a goal if I feel it is important enough. The discipline of writing has also impacted other areas of my life: my health, my exercise, my friendships and my self-belief, have all benefited from the habit of putting words on the page.

I have been honest, and in some cases, I know that this honesty may bring hurt to people I love or loved. This is not my intention, I did not write to blame people or air dirty laundry, but I needed to be honest with myself, 100%. Because if I was not, then what would I learn and how would I get better? I vowed that I would not hold myself back, so I have not.

If you are one of the people who are upset by my words, then I can only apologise and offer my love. I ask that you read the lessons I have learnt from the events, rather than the event itself, and you look at the person you have helped create, rather than the one who you hurt or who hurt you.

I would also like to thank all of the people who have taught me how I don't want to be. Sometimes, we strive to find the positive role model, only to learn the most from a very negative influence in our lives. I have had people teach me how not to lead, how not to support a friend, and how to keep someone small and scared. I love and thank each of these individuals for the divine lessons you have given me.

I would like to thank Andrew Dyckhoff, Giles Hutchins and Suhail Mirza for their endorsements and on-going support and belief. They are all Love Leaders in their own rights, and you can explore their work further at:

- Suhail Mirza - www.thesuhailmirza.com

- Andrew Dyckhoff - www.linkedin.com/in/ andrew-dyckhoff-0236a11

- Giles Hutchins - http://www.gileshutchins.com/

I would also like to thank Katie Hatfield for an amazing job at proofreading a book written by a dyslexic who uses American and English grammar and punctuation interchangeably. Never an easy task, but she did it with grace and speed.

A shout out to Maciek at Oxford Atelier who followed me around Oxford with a camera and managed to capture some great images with a smile.

ABOUT THE AUTHOR

Helen feels it is her mission to empower people to become the best they can be; to become happy, fulfilled and connected. In over 20 years working in corporate and SME environments, Helen has discovered that empowering people is the true mark of a leader, not chasing top line growth. Although she has found, over and over, that by leading and empowering people, sustainable growth happens naturally.

Helen has spent years working with teams and individuals, across the world, to help them deliver the best performance they can give and to learn to fulfil their potential, whatever that may be. She has done this by leading global teams, delivering training and coaching, and mentoring individuals to personal and professional growth.

Over the years, Helen has developed a curiosity to understand what makes her and others tick, and to help them become better leaders in the workplace by learning to care and love their teams.

Helen is not a theorist; she practices what she has learnt and what she teaches every day. Helen also sees herself as a perpetual student, knowing that every interaction, be it with international thought leaders or her own children, is an opportunity to grow, learn and become better at loving yourself and others.

Helen has spoken at events across the world for some of the world's largest companies, she has trained hundreds of people around the world and runs her own successful consulting business.

Helen is available for coaching, webinars, seminars and speaking events. She also runs online courses on www.helen honisett.com

• • •

Visit www.helenhonisett.com for
courses and supporting videos

LEAD WITH LOVE

UNITE & BUILD HIGH-PERFORMING TEAMS WITH LOVE, TRUST & INTEGRITY

Printed in Great
Britain
by Amazon